Copyright © 2016 Chantel Clickett

All rights reserved.

ISBN: 9781536876826

Season

[**see**-z*uh* n]

Noun: A period of time delineated by weather patterns and daylight.
Spring, summer, fall, winter, interval, hiatus, term, spell

Verb: To acclimatize, prepare.
Harden, toughen, temper, strengthen, discipline, steel

Verb: To add flavor.
Infuse, imbue, impart, color, spice, leaven, lace

Chantel Clickett

Seasons

Another grey day. As if the sky has melted the clouds and become an ashen soup of slush and grit. The crystal flakes that drift about beyond the window have lost their glitter, the magic of the holidays buried beneath the leaden weight of frozen snow. It always seems that winter becomes a petulant child this time of year; vacillating between tantrums and exhaustion, dragging his feet and clutching at the world with claws of fractured ice.

I dream of spring. I hear delicious whispers of warmth that trace patterns upon my flesh in the night and wake grumpily to the same arctic world I kissed goodnight the eve before. I want to nap. I want to sulk. I want to move south. Sometimes I wonder what it would be like to live in a climate without the radical seasonal changes found here in Pennsylvania. The pale green of spring that gives way to the lush sensuality of summer that burns itself out in a rush of copper and ruby and gold before the alabaster silence falls. The calendar flips, the clock ticks, and if you endure - hold your breath and pace and wait, another season is just weeks away.

And such is life really, isn't it? Some seasons gloriously grand, some barren. There are islands of paradise and deserts hellishly dry; monsoons and hurricanes and floods that threaten to drown. Fields of topaz wonder that stretch as far as you can see. Days of darkness, days of bliss. Sometimes you can anticipate the season ahead; hovering on the edge of the diving board, the anticipation intoxicating in itself. Sometimes it's an ambush, slamming you to the ground with enough force to crack your bones and knock the air from your lungs. Seasons of love, of despair, of wealth or starvation. Seasons of colourless stagnation and ones of spectacular bloom. Some cause permanent scaring, some heal. Some strip you naked and bare. Some teach you to fly.

It's nearly spring, can you feel it? As if the earth is stirring, the ground thirsty, poised on the brink of something undiscovered and succulent. I'm here, crossing my fingers, holding my breath, and hoping....

Spring

Hope is the dream of a soul awake.
French Proverb

In the spring, at the end of the day, you should smell like dirt.
Margaret Atwood

Pressed

The new year has arrived, slicing through the post-Christmas garland with atomic fireworks and showers of champagne and glitz. For nearly a week it felt like spring but the bitter cold has returned, shrouding the night in ice and mist. The glitter and twinkle have been packed away in old brown hat boxes and stacked neatly in the attic; green and red tablecloths nestled in with strands of holly and mistletoe and the antique silver star I adore. I'm still amazed at the holiday wonderland that slumbers quietly beneath the eves all summer long, broiling in the heat as it waits. Such magic that in a single day the house is transformed with fairy lights and pine boughs and the aroma of clove and spice. The excitement builds... gingerbread houses, foamy egg nog, crystal snowflakes hung from the chandelier.

Perhaps the real wonder is how quickly the Christmas cheer that has surrounded us for nearly two months can be whisked out of sight in mere hours. The house seems to echo a bit, empty rafters and pale shadows. Either way, here I stand at my ironing board. The old blue cover frayed and stained at one end from spilled coffee on a hurried morning. Ivory damask with a lovely mossy fern pattern lies piled before me; a new season, a new tablecloth.

Tiny flakes of white dance past the window as the hiss of the iron fills the room. Steam rises, the pale cloth smoothing beneath the ferrous plate, deliciously warm to my cool finger tips. The rhythmic pass back and forth quiets my scattered mind and I find myself thinking of wrinkles.

Sometimes it seems that a significant amount of my time is spent in this quest to eradicate them. Tablecloths and napkins, pants and soft cotton dresses; the crisp white shirts my husband wears to work. Curtains after a wash, the scarf that matches my raincoat, the skin about my eyes. Who decided the lines resulting from decades of laughter should be injected or sanded or peeled from my face? Does it make me look younger or just that I haven't a sense of humor? Would the world pause if the napkins had furled edges?

I've made no new resolutions this year. Being healthy and loving madly seem to cover just about everything for me, but perhaps I will think more about these wrinkles in my life. Perhaps as they are natural and lovely in their sweet crinkly way...perhaps this is a battle I shall concede.

Beyond

I heard a song the other day with the lyrics, "I'm moving beyond emotion, I'm standing on belief." I've searched for the song to no avail. It was a flash of lightening and then gone, yet its jagged imprint, vivid white against the obsidian of a night sky, has lingered. The words have echoed repeatedly through my thoughts, battling the mists of hurt and fear in my mind. Webby fingers of surprising strength, these are, threatening to strangle the choice and truth from my heart.

Emotions are powerful. Saturated and dense, thick with voices so loud they fill every crack and crevice within us. Elemental, they can whisper along our skin awakening within us passions glorious; or surge into a tsunami of titanic proportions, plunging us below the surface as we struggle for air. Emotions can seep from our minds to our hearts, invading our souls if we are not vigilant. A soul run purely on emotion enters dangerous territory.

Belief is different. Chosen. Built. Through experience, over time, drenched in our graphic humanity. *A conviction, a confidence in the truth or existence of something not immediately susceptible to rigorous proof,* the definition reads. Foundations that we live and breathe and walk upon; our beliefs are the stone of us, standing within the hurricane.

The seasonal change burgeoning around me reassures me of the cyclical nature of life. Dawn and then dusk and dawn again, no matter how dark the night. Storms and then sunshine, death and birth. The frigidity of winter eventually is won over by the warm wiles of spring. There is joy and then anger and sorrow and grief. Quiet solitude. Discovery, possibilities, and joy again. This permeates the lives of my children, my marriage, the battles that rage within me at times; as well as the world I've watched spilled out across the screen of our media this week, agony and suffering painting everything in shades of red and black. So much senseless anguish and death.

I have felt pain so deep I thought it would cleave me in two. Have been chased by fears that follow me wretchedly into my dreams, inescapable. Grief that sought to drown my soul...emotions that were waves threatening to wash away the shore.

But I *believe*.

In goodness.
In forgiveness and beginnings and strength.
In hope.
In healing.

No matter where you may be, step past the emotions. Choose your direction. Move beyond.

Onions

I'd had a rough day, I'd been sued. For someone who takes life and responsibility and respect as fervently as I do - to find oneself in this situation is unthinkable. That's what ex's are for. Needless to say, I won. I had proof in black and white and as the judge uttered the words, "waste of the court's time" I had the supremely euphoric sensation of warmth and absolution flood my taut limbs. Consummate relief, exoneration.

That night, as I lay in the arms of my husband, we spoke of life. We've both been through so much; enough it seems, to fill more than one lifetime. Do you ever feel that way? All my yesterdays and once-upon-a-times don't really add up, they somehow equal more than their sum of parts and it isn't necessarily comfortable. Carl Sandburg was the original Shrek poet. "Life is like an onion, you peel it off one layer at a time and sometimes you weep." I rather like the movie's interpretation, although I must admit that I am helplessly in love with onions. Sautéed until soft and juicy, caramelized dreamily and delicious; crisp with cheese and crusty bread. Daily I slice and chop and segment; stews, roasts, chili, risotto. Omelets, fajitas, egg rolls - seriously, onions are in everything! Their succulent layers sweet and spicy and sometimes hot, and sometimes rotten.

"People are like onions...." Our layers are, well, there. To be seen or shared or hidden; sometimes sliced away and put to compost as we re-invent ourselves after a culinary disaster of monstrous proportions. Uncommonly, the translucent reality of a life lived honestly reveals all, but ever so rare. More often, when there is so much, mountains done right and epochs done wrong, we're left trying to decipher, *what is the truth of us?*

Are we merely a sum of our layers? I asked my husband, "What if no one knew what I have done? Where I've been? Would it change how they feel about me?"

What if there was no…

"My father was a treasury agent and I was raised on a farm without a television and drank only goat milk."

"I spend hours in my studio painting my dreams so I won't forget them."

"We had a pet bobcat when I was a child that bit me in the neck."

"I can make cheese."

"I was a missionary in Guatemala; I worked in health clinics and orphanages and bathed in a river with snakes."

"I was the executive director of....but I also once worked in Hardees as the Fry Girl."

"My first marriage failed."

What if no one knew? If I was just...me. Am I merely an onion? Are you? I want to be loved and appreciated not just for where I've been or what I've done because there have been so many mistakes along the way. Dear Lord, the things we hide, even from ourselves; my triumphs have been marvelous, and my failures staggering. In between, I have grown. You hear often, "listen more, speak less" and this is my intention. For where I have been, the stories I could tell...perhaps I need to just stop. I am me. Not the past, not even what I might become. Just me. Is that enough?

Flirtation Nation

I've recently been accused of being a flirt, a rather large one at that. Moi? Yet unintentionally I've acquired a stalker most persistent and thus, tragically, I've lost my grocery store. *Do you know how traumatic that is??* Dammit, I knew where the turnips were! The coffee was in isle three and they had a particular kind of herbilicious brie I'd consider playing truth-or-dare for...and then I ruined it.

"How could this happen?" you ask. With a COMPLIMENT! A measly, weasly completely normal compliment! Except apparently someone has changed "the rules" and I missed the twitter or download or version III or whatever. This supposed "marriage proposal" of a compliment occurred in the checkout line. Twenty minutes of perusing the smashing array of vapid magazine covers and catching up on the latest of who's sleeping with who while adopting children after plastic surgery gone awry in Uruguay had left me at a loss and the sweet cooing of this darling baby in the buggy next to me was a welcome distraction.

There was a smile and a bit of drool combined with the foot kick and a squeal - a dead ringer move for stealing any heart - and I giggled right back! She laughed and I laughed and then glancing up at dad-e-o I commented, "She's really quite charming!" Wouldn't you know it, unbeknownst to me, this particular phrase has been upgraded from "casual conversation" to "hussy pick-me-up." Dear Saint Jehosophat and his pet clown, he followed me to my car! Two days later he chased me down the dairy isle inquiring how to pick yogurt. He even came into "Tampon Alley" with a toothy grin causing utter panic and I fled, leaving my buns woefully behind.

However, when regaling pals with this tragic tale, I was informed most readily by said pals that it is now actually written in "How to get a date" books: *Phase 1. Grocery store conversation.* AHHHHH! Do you mean to tell me that the "was it still raining when you came in?" is now a request to crash happy hour? "That looks like a fabulous melon" might get you slapped, and "oops, you dropped your crackers" is storefront foreplay?? Can someone please send me a new copy of these rules? Does this apply to...say, the Verizon store? *(I am SO re-thinking voicing my desire for "upgraded attachments")* What about the mall? Can I still ask for double cream in my coffee or will I be labeled as a sex addict for life? I've put off getting the oil changed in the car indefinitely. Somehow I'm certain "Please sir, will you check my fluids and lube the chassy?" is not going to end well....

Wanting To Be Wanted

I rescue things. From the time I was small, I've known this was my calling. When I was seven, I discovered a stray egg beside the edge of our hayloft. This was not uncommon as we had Guinea fowl amongst our flock of chickens and these fly quite well, thus roaming the farm stealing grain from the goats and teasing the dogs. Most evenings they would return to the hen yard, but every once in a while, we'd find an egg somewhere else.

This particular time, I simply tossed the egg into a compost pile and kept heaving bales up onto the wheelbarrow to be taken to the horses. Hours later, a casual glance caught movement in the pile. Further inspection revealed the trembling egg had cracked...a tiny beak had forced its way through. Knowing that for an egg to hatch, it must be incubated by a dedicated mother for nearly a month and this rarely happens for a single egg; I found myself on my belly worming my way up beneath the hay barn, scraping my cheek on the gravel as I felt around in the dark for the errant nest. My fingers brushed smooth shell and I wrapped my hand around the warm egg, and then jerked back with a yelp and a thump of my skull on the frame above me when my finger was bitten.

We had huge black carpenter ants in Colorado, an inch long with jaws large enough to draw blood should they catch a hold of you. I used to pick them up with my fingers, one by one, and let them clamp onto a piece of paper - so tightly that when I pulled them away it would pop their little heads off. Imagine a piece of stationary with a whole row of ant heads along the top - oh, the creativity of a bored farm girl! After retrieving a pair of gloves and a flashlight from the house, I once again wiggled my way up to the nest and collected seven more eggs in various stages of hatching. They were filled will hungry black ants tearing at the damp feathers and flesh of the hatchlings.

I remember my mother's sigh as I burst into the kitchen, her eyes softening as she saw my distress. She set aside her baking and we spent the next half an hour huddled over the eggs with tweezers, pulling the inky carnivorous insects from the fledgling peeps. We nestled the still partially shelled eggs in a towel lined pie tin and my mother set the oven at 85*. I knelt there on the floor for the next two hours, peering through the cracked door anxiously waiting for the chicks to emerge. I have no idea why their mother abandoned them to such a terrible fate, but now, I wanted them to live like I never had wanted anything before. Six survived and I named them all, but my favorite was Martha who followed me around like a puppy.

Now I have decades of rescuing behind me. Sometimes kittens, sometimes people; but not just the living call my name. Furniture and coat racks and long forgotten paintings left in dark webby corners of old attics whisper to me. I almost feel they have voices, crying out to be wanted - by anyone. At times I fear this has been just my own projection, as I have felt the same so often. I think most of us are created with this need to love and be loved; it's an ache that lies woven into the very fabric of our soul. It causes us to be reckless, to dash headlong into madness flinging our reservations away as we pursue it. And somehow, despite the catastrophes of the heart these ardent passions create; after the anguish, we seek to be desired once more.

    Did the antique desk with the book shelf attached call my name as we passed it lonely on the sidewalk, its legs cracked and broken? Perhaps. Perhaps I just saw myself within its damaged hulk. Last summer in the August heat, I bent over it, sawdust sticking to my arms and back as I smoothed out the edges with sandpaper, removing the bubbled finish. I rubbed walnut warmth back into the old panels, stain tinging my fingers dark for days. Carefully I cleaned the tarnish from the hinges and returned them to their divots. My husband glued the legs back together and crouched in the grass, I covered the glue with pigment, masking the defects from all but the closest of inspections.

    It now rests in the corner of our attic library. A decanter of whiskey, several bottles of wine, and a selection of glasses fill its shelves. Guests have marveled at it, amazed such a splendid piece could be left out for rubbish. In the same room is the poker table I made from the neighbor's weathered discard; the end console I resealed holds the hand-carved chess set smuggled home from Guatemala wrapped in my lingerie. As I sit in the quiet, surrounded by hundreds of old books I've amassed from damp garage sales and second hand stores, the room seems almost to breathe, the serenity tangible. Once more, they are wanted.

I've Lost My Today, Have You Seen It?

Lately I've found myself evaluating. It's a bit of a process, must say, to assess, to survey the property and consider. You see, I think there is an epidemic going round. It may sound strange, but an epidemic of tomorrow. The funny thing, is that I feel that it began with an epidemic of yesterday.

I have a pet peeve that at times erupts in the most awkward of circumstances. It's those people that continually harangue about what *should* have been. What might have, what could have or would have been *if only*... In my humble opinion, when the ink is on the paper, this has *absolutely no value*. Ziltch. Repetitive clamoring over the job she almost got, the date he should have had, or what happened at last year's holiday bash that wrecked my neighbor's shot at a raise - well, it's over. The only thing that truly matters, is what IS. I do not want to hear what a great doctor you *would have made*...but now you're a stripper. Seriously.

I suppose it makes my heart ache a bit, for those souls that live by re-living. They miss out on so much and seem perpetually starved, as if they've never tasted the delicious thrill of what is right here. Is life so disappointing? Can it hinge so imperatively on past choices or events, that recovery is impossible? Did you know, there are entire books written on what to do with lemons!

But then, we rebounded. The oceanic surge of Oprahesque promise and Philenthropic *(ha, I slay me!)* hope has nearly asphyxiated us with tomorrow. Bulging eyes and blue veins throbbing, we are clutching the future with desperate hands, a death grip on aspiration. For we have believed a lie: that we can have it all.

It's a lovely lie. A cozy, soft, tender lie. It's wrapped in tasty layers of potential and possibility and frosted with lottery-ticket glaze. Anything could happen, right? Pretty Woman taught me that. But this lie is a devastating thief. Such a nimble one, nearly invisible, we don't even suspect that he's there, in the room with us, stealing the real priceless jewel. Our today.

I'm truly not insane and I don't mean to imply that we should never plan or prepare for tomorrow - grocery shopping every day would drain me before I'd even begun to prepare the feast! However, I've known so many people, who are *living* for tomorrow. "When I get a raise...when we buy a house...when I graduate, when I'm skinny, when I'm married...." These things are indeed there, just up ahead....but not today.

Today is splendid. Today is real, flavored with saffron and orange zest and opportunity. Wrap your arms around it and embrace the astonishing miracle that is right *now*.

Kindness and Cucumbers

An older gentleman changed my day today. All by himself, in less than the time it takes to sneeze. It happened at the banana table, across from the avocados. I was rummaging around for a nice green bunch as those are the household favorites, and a cart pulled up alongside me. I glanced over. He was in his late 60's I'd say, a little gray but neat and tidy in that comforting way I remember my grandfather being. He was looking at me. I blush easily and so, looked down. He said,

"You have such beautiful hair. My wife had hair like that....have a nice day." He smiled, I smiled back.

"Thank you." Turning the corner just past the bakery, he was gone. I picked out cucumbers and tomatoes. And kept smiling.

It hadn't been a particularly good day. Full of my own doubts and accusations, fears and worries; the skies were black and it was pouring which makes my bones feel as if they're being twisted inside my flesh. Grocery shopping on such days leaves much to be desired, but three boys under 13 make it necessary lest you find teeth marks in the woodwork and missing carpeting. It was just one sentence, and I was smiling.

Recently I seem surrounded by stories of the poverty and desperate need in the world. Commercials on television with starving children and beaten dogs, unexpected suicides haunting the headlines, violence between neighbors shattering everyone involved. Sometimes it's as if the darkness within us is an ocean, vast and deep. How can we, how can *anyone* make a difference in an ocean?

After my years in Guatemala and Mexico, I went to Philadelphia. While my time spent within the walls of orphanages and health clinics in foreign lands was amazing; nothing - not even those months on a rope and stick cot, the legs sprayed with Raid to keep the tarantulas off in the jungle - *nothing* prepared me for the culture shock I was to experience in Philly. We lived in an old warehouse on Kensington Avenue; the bad part of Kensington, under the El. (*elevated train*) Rusted razor wire ran in spiky loops across the tops of our fences and walls. I could never tell if we were being kept in, or others, out. There were four locks of various natures on the front door, three on the back, and a wrought iron grid over every window. Two bullet holes in the paneling near the television seemed to watch us even as we watched it.

'Daily Bread' was the name of our soup kitchen. Lines would stretch out for blocks when the temperature plummeted close to zero; lines of broken hearts and damaged souls. To prevent the arrogance that can come with mission and outreach work if unchecked, once a week we were all required to dress in our grubbiest, sans lipstick and scent, and stand in line among those we normally served. Pick up a tray, a handful of water-spotted silverware, shuffle our way along, eat whatever was served. We sat, side by side, with the shattered. Crammed onto benches, my thigh pressed against one wearing jeans that hadn't been washed in over a month; and I listened to the wearer tell me he used to be a banker. He had lived on the other side of town in a tall green house with his wife and two daughters, Susannah and Margaret. There had been a holiday party at the office that ran late and someone had brought a crack pipe. Three years later he was eating scrambled eggs and pickles next to me.

The depth of this sore, this cancer, was overwhelming. Sometimes I couldn't breathe for it; this was *here*, in *my* country. Blocks on end of devastated people...and above us, trains of suit-wearers; new heels and linen pants and leather briefcases. Faces looking down; looking, but never seeing. That year I confronted many of my own preconceived notions; the idea that if they really *wanted* out, these people just had to work harder to get out. That they had somehow, through a series of unfortunate events, chosen this.

Juanita changed that. Juanita was a whore. An ugly whore. She sold herself for just five dollars, *can you imagine?* That's how much a rock of crack cost two streets over, behind the derelict grocery store with the crooked sign. One night there was banging on our front door. We had a rule about not opening it after a certain hour but there was a desperation in this pounding, it shook the door frame itself. It was Juanita, she had a black eye. I made hot chocolate.

The rest of the house slept as we ate reheated mac & cheese, watched Wheel of Fortune reruns, and talked. Somewhere near dawn she told me how she had become a prostitute. She had been sold to a man by her mother when she was seven, and then given drugs to manage the trauma. Juanita never had a choice or a chance. I pulled a blanket up over her skeletal arms after she fell asleep on the couch and I wept. Never before had my blessed and protected life seemed so terribly unfair.

Juanita stayed on our couch often after that. Once when she was high I had to turn her away, but she came by the next afternoon with a donut for me and apologized. We sat on the curb, cold sunshine on our cheeks and powdered sugar on our fingers. I told her I was scheduled to leave the next day. She smiled. Do you know what she said?

"Aww, Chantel, you such an angel I knowed I couldn't have you all to myself. You got other lives to touch." And she was *happy* for me. I wept again, my tears icy in the wind. She helped me pack my tattered boxes into the truck the following morning. She smelled like strawberry lip gloss when I hugged her. Juanita waved like mad as we drove away, the bald spots on her head gleaming in the sun. I waved back; hoping, praying I made some kind of difference in her life.

I returned to life as I knew it. A paying job, dinners at with napkins, cable tv. However, I lost many friends. Even the relationships within my family were different; for I was not the Chantel that everyone kissed goodbye and joked with about living out of two boxes for so long. No, that Chantel didn't ever come back. I did. Humbled and bruised, with very different eyes. I'd seen behind the curtain and lost Peter Pan for good; Juanita had come to live within my heart in his place.

Since then life hasn't fallen quite so neatly in the rows I'd planned. It's unfolded with more creases, sometimes holes I've vainly tried to patch. But those years in some of the darkest and most challenging places - they changed the mother I am. They changed my art and my voice, the colors I see. They altered the neighbor I've become, they laid the foundation for the daycare centers I ran. They shaped the wife and woman that types these words.

That is what kindness does. It doesn't necessarily dry up the ocean, but it permanently transforms the mind and soul of the *giver*. And *every life they come into contact with after*. Kindness isn't about curing the disease, but changing a day. One day can alter the course of a lifetime.

Or just make someone smile, as they pick out cucumbers.

Gesso

Liquid white forgiveness. Thick, warm; it drapes my canvases in layers of love, erasing the smeared and awkward. The crooked, the ugly, the failures. Plaster grace, gypsum clemency. I have canvases that have 3, 4…6 different paintings sleeping beneath the one that was finally accepted, hung, and purchased by someone it spoke to. The gentleman from Florida that took three of my forest series home with him last week has no idea that lying under the graceful branches of that shady path is a blackened thing. Angry. Two in the morning and four whiskeys and rage…it slumbers now in the quiet of the woods.

I've come to treasure that bottle of ivory exoneration. The morning after the fight or disappointment or defeat; when the tears have passed and the dappled glow of dawn filters through the curtains, I can start again. Mistakes…we all make them. Some of the landslide errors I've committed have decimated mountains. Tsunamis that have wiped my triumphs from the map, earthquake misjudgments leaving sinkholes and black chasms in my life. I've wept rivers, mashing palms into my eye sockets till there were bruises, redefining regret.

Yet we breathe. The sun rises, the wind blows. Somehow the grass keeps growing and the dog needs fed and you pay the electric bill. We go on. So tell me, why do I still stumble so? You'd think that I'd learn to leave the light on, to watch my step. Sometimes I feel my snarls are simply hunkered down beneath the bed, festering. Am I going blind?

Where is the gesso for life? Is there a magic pigment that will turn my monsters into ghosts? Take away their claws and give them fluff instead of fangs? I have faced them, I have paid. I am tired. It's not a quest for euphoria, I assure you. I'd settle for peace. I've known the mercy of the Lord, the compassion of friends - somehow though, the monsters are still there. Perhaps they live inside me.

It's begun to snow again. Alabaster flakes blanket the mud and barren branches that ring the yard...gesso from the sky.

Breath

Dusk was falling outside the window over my white porcelain kitchen sink. Icy frost etched patterns of lace around the edges of the glass, nearly hiding the chip in the corner, testimony to some long forgotten flying rock and a child's poor aim. Thin white clouds painted orange with the last of the sun's rays scuttled across the slate sky, seeming to run from the approaching night. I hummed along with Diana Krall while my buttered fingers twisted the soft dough into knots, the scent of rosemary and roasted garlic mingling with the stew simmering on the stove.

I heard him come in. Lately, my husband has made it home earlier than usual...I think the arctic freeze of February makes home all that much more irresistible, with its warmth and promised feast - well, that and things at work have settled some. The clink of keys on the bar, the hiss of a coat's zipper, footsteps behind me. His hands on my waist, sliding around, make me laugh as I am helplessly entangled with the bread. His chest against my back, he presses his face into my neck and the heat of his breath slides across the soft skin behind my ear...heaven.

My first marriage - when we slept at night, he didn't like to be touched. And I wasn't allowed to breathe on him. I should have known then it was never going to work out. I am such a...physical person. It is within the nature of my very cells, I believe, to touch. I ache to be touched. Perhaps it is something I've cultivated, but I am blessed to have teenage boys that still hug me several times a day, a slew of affectionate friends - cheek kissing and hand holding and curling up together to watch a movie. Human contact is essential for me. I wither without it.

Most intimate of all, is breath. That moment just before his lips trace the curve of my shoulder...the tingle of it across wet skin...the taste of him just before we kiss. The other night he whispered, "I love your breath" in the flicker of candlelight. After making love, entwined such as to not know where your flesh ends and theirs begins. When two souls have drunk their fill of each other, savored and explored and relished...saturated. I smiled and raised my head from his chest, stopping millimeters from his lips, I felt him breathe in when I exhaled...

"I know."

Mosaic

Ice is falling from the sky today. Clouds of lead scatter frozen glitter across the world outside my window, I can hear it patter against the glass. The multiplicity that is spring never ceases to amaze as this day is nearly polar of one just a few weeks past when balmy breezes and sun-filled skies oversaw the cleaning of my potting bench; the stacking of clay vessels, inventory of seeds and soil and plans begun. I swept the front porch and replaced the urns which are begging for fledgling ferns once winter has truly taken his leave. Removing the now shriveled chives and thyme that passed away beneath ivory blankets of snow, I organized the lanterns, wiped down chairs and tables in anticipation of lengthening evenings, warmer winds, and mug of tea sipped while the children play hockey in the street.

At the far end of the porch, where I like to sit and read, is a table. My table. I found it abandoned on the curb, rusted and put out for the trash. Grinning ear to ear, I was already making plans as I wedged it into the back seat of the car; a summer project unfolding with a coat of black paint, and the bag of broken glass I'd gotten for a quarter at a yard sale. I'd never tiled anything other than the floor in the entryway of our house, and that was all numbered and logical. This was madness with razor sharp edges.

I remember the sun warm on my bare shoulders, my hair tied up but managing to escape anyway in long pieces that blew about in the summer air. Music drifted out from the double front doors that are always left open when weather permits, Hazel dozed upon the steps, her floppy ears at rest as she snoozed in the shade. I knelt on the cement walk and carefully covered bits of blue and green, like chips of the sky and sea, with an old kitchen cloth. The hammer clutched in my hand, its leather grip leaving ridges in the flesh of my palm, I shattered them. Sawyer, my eldest son, came out and sat on the grass beside me.

"Can I try?" he asked.

"Of course, love," I said, "just be sure to cover the glass with the towel so we don't get pieces in the yard." He followed instructions, raised his arm, and pulverized it to dust. "Whoa!" I laughed, "Not so hard or I won't have anything left to glue!" He grinned and we worked together for another twenty minutes or so before he dashed off to play with his brothers. I carefully picked up the pieces and returned to the naked table.

I had some general idea of what I'd like to see, but nothing truly planned. I spread the paste, and placed the first piece. Then the second, and the third. It seemed the ocean spilled out over that table, held together with glue and some of my own blood smeared from tiny nicks and cuts; grimly jagged, that glass was. I had to sort through the fractured remains, searching for one that was triangular, square...flat on top and round on the bottom. As the design unfolded, my needs were more and more specific. Back to the walk and now choosing carefully, I tapped. I chiseled. Microscopic adjustments, precise movement...deliberate splintering.

I ran out of flat glass. Had to improvise with odds and ends found about the house. Patiently I worked the black grout between the knifelike rivulets, dark sand gritty beneath my nails. Certainly, it resembles nothing machine made, imperfection is its claim to beauty. Unique and slightly uncentered, much as I.

    I found myself tracing the now passive bits of glass, their edges muted, lethality expunged. Oh, how life has chiseled me. I find astonishing comfort in this thought. There is marvelous beauty in this life we all share; a tapestry of love and agony, death and birth and sunlight on still ponds. Each of us a part, shaped by forces greater than ourselves. Sculpted. Sometimes just a sanding of the rough, sometimes surgery of the soul. But together, our broken bits glinting in the light....

    We are lovely indeed.

Reflections

The heat of the oven is delicious on my skin. My kitchen, with its massive antediluvian window and three outside walls, tends to be one of the coldest rooms in the house, thus leading to a near perpetual parade of fresh breads and cookies, roasts and creamy casseroles, any possible excuse I can come up with to keep the oven burning as we persevere through snow and sleet. Warm air swirls in drafts around me, the scent of rosemary and garlic doing battle with Jack Frost as he clings to the window glass. One hip resting against the counter, the edge of the porcelain sink cool beneath my fingers...and night slowly swallowed the day.

When was the last time you actually watched, minute by minute, the evening arrive? Dusk, with her lovely cloak of grey, gently drapes the world in silver; her darkness eclipsing the skeletal trees, shrouding the back fence, veiling the sky until the window holds nothing more than a dim reflection of the small warm kitchen and the woman within. So still, she stands. Auburn hair framing pale skin. The curve of my neck, the shadow of a collar bone disappearing under white cotton, the glitter of a silver chain.

Is that what I look like? To the trees outside? The rising moon? What do they see? Every morning I face that woman, run a brush through her hair, blacken her lashes, slide color across her lips. But do you know, *we never truly see ourselves*...only our reflections. And as so much of vision is actually perception, woven with expectations, memories and hope, rather than strictly observation; I fear I see more...or possibly less, in that reflection than most. Flaws, inadequacy, tremendous potential and crushing failure; joy and grief and thirst. Her green eyes gaze back at me, a flat image on mirrored glass; no breath, no warmth, no blood within. Not me...a reflection.

    The other day a friend stopped by for a visit and we sat with cups of tea, feet curled beneath us on the old leather couch in the living room. She smiled at the plants that drape from the mantle and the edge of the buffet, the bird's nest woven with dried grass and filled with painted eggs that rests on the dining room table, surrounded by river stones.

    "I'd know this was your house even if it were my first time here," she said, "Just by the scent of it....I can see you everywhere, every room reflects you." I suppose that makes sense, my home is another reflection of me - but one of mingled proportions for others are here too. Finger painted flowers on the wall in the kitchen, brought home with love when my eldest was merely seven, six years past now. End tables that arrived with my husband, the pedal organ from the 1800's that he and I bought together and refurbished into a bar; paintings signed by my grandmother, the piano from my great grandfather, all jumbled together. I wonder what my home says about me; what would a stranger know passing within these walls... what secrets revealed?

    I can hear the boys now, downstairs. Laughter echoing up through the vents, a new James Bond video game their latest thrill. A co-worker told me last week when the boys came with my husband to pick me up from the office; that they walked like me. I had no idea. Our children divulge worlds about us, astonishingly accurate reflections of who we really are. Our beliefs and foundations stripped bare of the veneer of speech and facade of accoutrements. Children are the truth of us.

Night has chased away the day now. Wine warms slowly in the glass beside me, casting fractured rays of garnet light as I write. I wonder at the verity of my soul...the reality of me. Am I found within the reflections?

Mattresses From Heaven

I just had a gallery opening. This means that I ate/breathed/slept in - and never quite removed all the paint on me for several weeks no matter how hard I scrubbed. This also means that things were a little....*tense* in our house. **ahem** For all you non-marrieds, this is code for "I was a total neurotic bee-otch running on caffeine and adrenaline who tested my husband's patience and made nothing but hot dogs for 14 days straight.

Gallery opening - rocked. Sold some. Breathe...it's all good. And then I crashed. Brain deadness in a delicious way, sleep, leftover wine, sleep more. So two days later and we're having this discussion about things that we've "meant to do" and just haven't gotten around to. Like my kid's bed. The boys were in bunkbeds but now that they have their own rooms - Sawyer has been crashin' on ye ole floor for a few months now. Not that he really cares - when you're ten, "camping" in your own room is cool. But we had the frame - just needed to get out and pick up a mattress…and drop a couple hundred bucks. Yeah, been dying to do that. And after the paintress-from-hell week we'd had; well, I just wasn't really in the mood.

So I did what every sweet darling woman would, I seduced my husband. Yes, you read that right. With a little sigh and wiggle and flutter of the eyelashes - oh, and I threw in suggestions of block buster and some rum and ordering wings and garlic bread.... mattress? What mattress? Let's hear it for sex, food, and entertainment!

The next day, hop in the caddie and hit the highway and...slam on the breaks.

"Did you see that?"

"See what?" Reverse. Miss the mile marker post.

"Um.....is that what I think it is??" A mattress. *A brand spankin' new, still-in-the-plastic, holy crap on a cracker (to quote my sister) twin mattress!* What do we do?? I mean, it's not like there's a missing mattress hotline, right? We stood there on the side of the road...cars whizzing by, blurred faces gawking at us as we hummed and hawed and decided to wait like 10 minutes in case someone came back for it. *(then I would have arm wrestled them)* And then...

Two freaks on the road high-fiving, whooping it up like crazy crack addicts as we just about wet ourselves laughing while trying to get this sucker into the trunk. I could fit 3 dead bodies in that Cadillac's rear end - and with enough jammin and slammin and a *very* handy bungee cord, we drove our fabulously free find home.

Um......God? Is there a car fairy?

Hell Has Another Name

Tuesday, March 9
Official Record.

Previously: Best Friend calls to initiate contact. Frivolous discussion about said friend's upcoming trip to Florida; beaches, swimsuits.... lovehandles.

"Um.....shall we go for a walk this week, to exercise a bit?" she says. "There's a park near my house with a lake."

"Sounds lovely! Tuesday perhaps?"

Now to be absolutely fair, BF did indeed casually mention that it was five miles. As I tear up about eight miles in twenty minutes on my stationary bike every other day or so, I thought very little of this.

I pick her up in my truck, we are dynamically jolly on our way to the lake. My, that is quite a lake, eh?

We arrive and park, stashing coats in the back seat as the sun is gloriously shining, warming the 43* air to a delusional "warm spring day." I glance about. The women in the parking lot are...a bit intimidating. Folks, I'm wearing jeans. And old tennies. A t-shirt with some bar logo on it and a sweater I often paint in - leaving it dabbed here and there with various pigment additions. These other women have apparently stepped out straight from Shape magazine. Glamorous athletic outfits with glowing piping and detail. Hell, they have matching shoes and headbands! *(when did flashdance come back in? Oh wait - those are ear warmers...)* They're flipping bouncy pony tails as they tuck designer ipods into tiny waistbands...I hate them.

Mile 1

Picturesque. Blazing sunshine glints off the ice, regal geese meandering through the grass, we stride; long steps and deep breaths. We throw back our heads and laugh, jaunting along, giggling at the construction guys that are actually getting into wet suits. *(for some reason they were going into the lake under the ice - um, insanity?)* Nonplussed, we parade on. The clouds are so fluffy...

Mile 2

Slight wheezing. BF requests that I slow down. So thoughtless of me! Of course, my dear - I'm six feet tall and darling Ag is five foot three, completely unfair there. We notice the geese rather stink. We chuckle as we comment that every runner passing us looks to be in pain. Ha, ha, what IS their problem? Is that a hill? My goodness.

Mile 3

The chafing begins. Perhaps they could post a warning, "G-strings are highly unrecommended for long ventures." There was that awkward sideways step with a hop as I try to inconspicuously grab the string through my jean pocket. Ag: "*That's* why they make active wear." Wench. Whose idea was this?

Mile 4

Oh. My. God. *gasp* "Is that the end of the lake?" Ummm....no. That's just where the trail takes off up the MOUNTAIN there and then bends to the right, circles around and then we have to go all the way back down the other side. Damn geese shit is *everywhere!* There is now a distinct burning sensation in my hip joints. I'm seriously considering hitch hiking. There is a nice mother and children walking a sweet dog coming our way. We're passing. I smile....perhaps it was more of a grimace as she immediately put one child behind her protectively. Ag: "She's got car keys around her neck! You grab the keys, I'll take out the kids and we'll drive back to our car!" Sheer panic on the woman's face. I smack Ag, "Quit scaring the pedestrians!" In the distance I hear the woman say, "Now THAT is why you should never talk to strangers!" Dear Lord, we've become today's lesson in stranger danger.

Mile 5

I'm now serious about hitching. My right calf has seized. I joke about a ride and some pervy old man with fake hair on a bench gets up, "Hey baby, I'll give you a ride." Ag: "Walk FASTER DAMMIT!" I consider replying, but I cannot breathe.

The parking lot

I'm dragging a leg. Ag sounds like a thrashing grouper. We're nearly crawling and she says, "I know this hair-brained idea was mine, but I'm the crazy one in this relationship here; you approved it! You're like MANAGEMENT!"

This morning I can hardly move. I made it down for coffee...and nearly had a seizure trying to put my socks on.

I'm firing management.

Persevere

The human being amazes me. Not for its capacity for creativity or beauty or science, not for advancement or achievement or depravity, but for its ability to endure.

Scar tissue. Twisted lumps of whitened flesh that feel nothing. Severed nerve endings dangle uselessly, sending no messages...communicating nothing. I have a rather smashing scar on my right bicep. I was flying a kite as a child and while laughing and looking up to the clouds as I was running - I crashed headlong into a barbed wire fence. The best thing about this particular macula is that as I lived on a farm, miles from the closest doctor, after the original trip to be stitched up, a return visit for the "snipping" was deemed unnecessary by dad. Perhaps it was a bit premature, but he thought the gash had healed well enough and sliced through the thread. It took a bit of yanking. Each and every spot that needle had pierced my skin, pulling filament behind, left a scar alongside the laceration. Quite Frankenstein, I assure you, looks great with a tan. *(and yes, I have told gawking strangers that I got it during a knife fight in Hong Kong...)*

I've known many over the years who, thanks to sports and motorcycles and teenage antics, boast of scars much greater than mine. Did it deter them? No. The physical pain that wrecked through their bodies at the time of the injury was soon forgotten. The alabaster disfigurement becoming a badge of glory worn with pride during future episodes of genius judgment. Some might say this ability to omit physical pain is the reason we actually give birth to more than one child. I still fly kites.

There are some scars, however, that are not so simply dismissed. They lay unseen, hidden beneath our pulsing flesh... jagged holes in our soul. These we do not boast about. They change the color of the air. Yet the agony, no matter how grievous, doesn't kill us. At some point we fear it might, and then the sun rises.

The human being places bare feet on the cold floor. There is dust on the nightstand. Icy water sluices over the sink, puddles about the base. The click of the medicine cabinet seems to echo. Stare at the bedroom doors across the hall...small heads and soft hearts sleeping there still. A teddy bear on the floor. Plug in the iron, drape the skirt over the pale blue stained board. Breathe. One step, then another. And then another.

Someone once said, "When you have no idea what to do, just do what comes next."

Planting

Thunder is rumbling across the sky sending shivers down my spine, how I do so love the storms of spring. Iron clouds of battleship grey undulate outside my window, rain sluicing down the glass even as it trembles, washing winter's touch from the surface of the world. Rain is a lovely thing. Its damp entrance does indeed make my bones ache but it accomplishes one thing that even my husband despairs to achieve - it makes me pause. Traps me inside, leaves the tools and stones and seeds outdoors...and I rest. At the moment, I'm rather relieved as the bruises have accumulated a bit faster than usual lately. Last week I spent seventeen hours on a ladder scraping, sanding and painting the porch ceiling a delicious dark chocolate to match the shutters. Painted the porch and rails, scrubbed the siding to a blinding white *(which I fear has been before our purchase of this place since last occurring)*, potted up the ferns, filled the hummingbird feeder and cleaned the grill in anticipation of long delicious evenings. I only fell off the ladder once. And then the roses arrived.

Frustrated with the anemic shrubs that crouched along the front of the house like anorexic tarantulas, I took the plunge and sent off for three rose bushes of a new variety: low on sun, blooms from spring through the crisp of fall, resistant to mold and spot - essentially heaven with honey colored petals. Did I mention that I've never planted roses before?

Tucked within the neat brown wrapping along with the rooted plants, was a small innocuous book, "How To Plant

Anything." Page twenty: Roses. Did you know a two foot wide, two foot deep hole dug into the earth for every plant is required? *(I certainly did not)* Fill the bottom with gravel for good drainage, mix the loam and soil and pile into a cone shape upon which you sill spread out the baby roots which have been soaking for a day....

Two hours past dinner, dusk not far off, I'm on my knees in the front yard. A tear in my jeans leaves smears of black and brown on my leg. My old Chuck Taylors slipping in the mud and grass, I lugged buckets of broken rocks to the edge of the now prepared *(holed)* brick edged flower bed. My husband came out to watch for a bit...."More than you anticipated, hmmm?" I think I panted an answer of a grunt, heaving dirt up onto the tarp I'd spread out to protect the lawn.

One neighbor offered root beer which my husband enjoyed, and another brought me a strawberry alcoholic beverage that I slurped down like a nine year-old with a slushy. *(we do have such lovely neighbors)* My back ached. The muscles in my arms were hard and felt like wire twisted too tight beneath my flesh as the leather gloves chafed the soft skin on the inside of my wrists. I had grit on my cheek and bits of grass in my hair, but as I held the already budding canes carefully still while gently pouring the soft dirt that smelled of life and wind and rain to cover roots that I whispered prayers of deep growth over, the satisfaction was nearly a flavor on my tongue. Such is planting.

Some of my earliest memories were of my mother in the garden. I remember watching the miracle of tiny black seeds sprouting into heads of cabbage and mountains of tomatoes and squash long before ever stepping a foot inside school. I think my first true love might have been dirt. The possibilities within the dark earth...ground well-tilled, aired out and tumbled with nutrients, fertile land within which to grow and flourish. Nourishment of the soul as well as the body whole.

It's work. It's painful. I've nine bruises, two scrapes, and a middle finger the color of dark plums due to a slipping shovel. But oh, the seeds we plant regardless; some with care, some without. In our children, our relationships, our futures. I look back and clearly see the years my garden was…lacking. My investment was terribly visible in the harvest. Sparse and dry. Perhaps this understanding comes with age? Watching a thought bulge into an idea and then unfold into a plan. Exertion and discipline and sweat. And then luscious, succulent fruit. Or maybe the recognition of a kindred soul, infused with time and kindness - and friendship follows. Journals written, talents explored, horizons challenged...

The air is heavy, saturated with rain and promise. What are you planting this spring?

I Should have Come With A Warning Label

I am a menace. To myself, that is. The rest of the planet is safe...well, unless you happen to be walking behind me close enough to catch a flailing arm as I attempt a hack-kneed swan dive in the middle of the sidewalk, complete with a set of shrieking howls resembling those of mating alley cats. And dear God help you if you are in front of me when I'm attempting to negotiate the spinny door at the hospital or board the escalator in the mall. *(stupid things should have harnesses)* There will be causalities. Why, you ask, do I provide such entertainment on a regular basis for the throngs that gather? Oh baby, I was born this way!

While reaching for the salad dressing the other night, I was stopped by my husband's,

"Oh my WORD honey, what did you DO to your hand?!?" I'm totally blank.

"Hmmm?" I ask.

"Look at your hand!" he points to the fingers clutching the blue cheese like I'm about to be robbed. Upon closer inspection, I began to count...two burns, a slice across my ring finger, my first knuckle was missing, and there is an inch and a half gash down the side of my palm. Admittedly, it was a hot mess.

"This is the new sexy." I told him.

I remember losing the knuckle while adjusting my stationary bike. *(imagine my husband laughing out loud as I'm attempting to explain this. "You got hurt riding a stationary bike?")* The gash was acquired while cleaning under the microwave which had a previously unknown broken plastic thingy that removed my flesh like Satan's melon baller - of course I irritate it every time I get my phone out of my pocket or put gloves on, so I've jacked it up even more. The rest? Not. A. Clue.

It's been like this forever. Today is my birthday and I have been a poster child for band aides and Neosporin for so long I should demand shares in the company! *(right now my left knee is a stunning rainbow of color as I dropped the largest drawer in the guest room dresser two days ago and caught it with my leg)* I think I've developed some kind of pain nerve memory block. Honestly, you could hold a gun to my head and demand to know how I bruised the entire back of my arm last week and *I would have to die*. I have NO recollection whatsoever! I fall UPstairs. I trip over carpets like a drunk ballerina with a death wish. I now have an escort that seems to follow me around Home Depot, I think they were worried there would be lawsuits.

Years ago I went to visit one of my best friends in Florida. It was to be a romp of a weekend; fly down on Friday, back on Sunday. I left a chipper, smiling girl with a bounce in her step. 48 hours later I returned with the skin missing from half my face *(scraped it along the bottom of a pool)*, limping *(pulled my hamstring in a wild game of cosmic bowling)*, and gasping like an emphysema commercial as I had caught some plague while guzzling the apartment complex pool water. I had to get shots. Missed a week of work to recover from that "two day girl get-a-way."

I couldn't watch the movie The Hangover. It was entirely too real. I own enough ace bandages to mummify a moose. I think we should have punch cards for the doctor's office: "nine visits and the tenth one is free" or at least you get a coffee…or a donut.

Bristled Regret

I've sat here staring at the keyboard for over thirty minutes. I've typed two sentences. Erased them both. I am...stumped, feel incapable of communicating my thoughts. The precipice of a chasm, completely unforeseen, that snuck up and sucker punched me on a splendid sunny afternoon.

First, I should say that most of you may think this ridiculous. But to each soul is its own solar system, the gravitational force that keeps the balance; that which maintains. As varied as the fish in the sea are the suns that ground each of us. I went upstairs today to finish a painting. It sold quickly but needed a signature, a touch or two, and a wire. I remember the tumult of the night I'd previously worked on it; a thunderstorm, heartache and a sick child. Interruption and hurry and comfort and...

I opened the window today. Soft breezes scented with lilacs and the color green drifted into the room along with the distant sound of dogs and arguing birds. I flipped the stereo on, chose, pushed play. Hazel settled with a bone to gnaw in the patch of sunlight that pooled on the floor while I piled my hair up and tied it with a scarf out of the way. Humming, I filled the chipped teapot I use for water....and saw it. My brush. *The* brush.

***She was shy, unsure. Timidly she stacked the paints and brushes on the scuffed black counter, blushing as she bungled it and tubes tumbled to the floor. He was older, totally "artistic," and miles out of her league. He smiled and held up a brush with a bright red

handle.

"This is a really good one." He said. It disappeared into the bag much as she did out the door, cheeks aglow, a checked-off class list clutched in a sweaty palm...***

Twenty years ago. I had a tool box I used as my art kit. The little compartments and trays were perfect for charcoals and pastels, graphite, erasers and paint. I remember the smell of the studios in college, blank paper and raw promise. I had absolutely no idea what I was doing. How does one find one's place, establish a root within a tangle of talent, and grow?

The years plummeted by, countries and oceans and lives changed. Do you know I painted the twenty-eight canvases for my first show in a windowless basement lit with three bare bulbs....and I was selling plasma to feed my toddler boys. My fingers rubbed the red paint from the brush handle, and forests fell upon fabric. I sold out.

Betrayal. Divorce. The red paint flaked and I composed skies and oceans and apocalyptic deserts. New love meant canvases of ferns and sunlight and rivers of liquid hope. The equator leveled.

I didn't rinse it. Twenty years, not a brush lost. And it was THE brush. Now stiff...rigor mortis. Bristles caked solid with forest pigment, the color of dark wet moss that drapes the ground, kneeling beneath kings and queens of bark. I was interrupted. I forgot. While I have dozens more, liners and fans and tapers and - there isn't a canvas with my name on it that hasn't felt the stroke of that brush. The handle had warped to fit my fingers. It's the only way I know to paint a sky.

Most mistakes can be absolved. Apologies and grace and even reparation made. The concrete can be replaced, right? Not always. Do you know, as my awareness of the dependence I had upon this particular brush dawned, I have searched for years for another. Twelve stores, four states. I laughed it off, knowing - absurdly arrogant - that I *never* forget to religiously cleanse my tools, the channels of my dreams into tangible reality. I am absolute. I am careful. I am...terribly human.

I have purchased over forty brushes in the last three years trying for one like it. Tonight I toast the final painting of my crimson brush. I actually sit here wondering if I can do the same with another. Perhaps that is madness to you, but hundreds of dollars trying to find one with the same grip, the sweep, the swirl and glide and hush...

In a day which held darkness and joy of such variety for so many, I am stilled by hairs congealed with neglect. Mine.

The Deliciousness of Dirt

Sometimes I can almost feel the calcification of my bones in the cold. It seeps into my tendons and muscles, permeating tissues, they petrify. And then one morning, shuffling to the car...a pause. What? A breeze? Not the acrid scrape of winter's breath, but something warm, soft, sweet. Time lapse photography would document the melting of snow, the green mist that crept across the yard - and perhaps the daily lightening of my steps. Secret smiles beneath the curtain of my hair as careful fingers plucked blackened leaves from tiny nubs, tulips and daffodils gasping for air. The brittle smack of tape and plastic peeled from the ancient 15 paned window in the dining room; the hand crank turns and glass glides and creamy sheer curtains billow into the room...sweet spring.

My knees are sore; the left one stained from the tear in my jeans. The sun was irresistible - and the light glow on my shoulder blades testifies to my careless abandonment of the sweater I ventured out in. Spaghetti tank straps have left ivory shadows behind. Ahhhh...the seduction. Dark and loamy, vital - the smell of soil. Alive. Plunging my hands deep into the bed, breaking clumps, churning the earth, burgeoning with the promise of basil and rosemary, fresh tomatoes, cucumber salad with prawns and dill.

Kneading the dirt, I wonder at the miracle that takes the dead, the digested, the waste of our lives and with heat and light and time creates the perfect medium for new growth. Last year's mistakes, miscalculations - become life. How often we miss this. Frantically I have tried to rearrange, reorder, rethink. Perhaps I have lost the marvel that is the garden. Renewal. Rebirth.

    My fingers seek out bits of tangled roots, the weeds of last season desperately clinging to the hope of invisibility. Have I let the weeds in my mind take root? The smallest of seeds can grab hold, invade. Do we evaluate our lives with the care that Home Depot assumes we take with our lawns? What do we cultivate, what do we thin? Our work, our homes....schedules, family, commitments. Do we plant the extravagant as well as the healthy? Mint and lavender and plums. Every garden is temporary. Each has a season. Casual hands bear spindly fruits. It's the careful heart, the attentive soul, the calloused palm, that reaps succulent bounty.

Within Your Grasp

"Your hair always looks so nice." she sighed, her voice slightly peevish with envy.

"Well, it doesn't look this way when I wake up!" I joked, attempting to shrug off the situation. She sighed again, touching her own dry brittle curls.

"It's just not fair!" So I began to cautiously explain that I use a ten minute conditioner on my hair twice a week and a balm in the morning to tame any frizz. Then I generally toss it up in a few hot rollers while I sip coffee and... "That's too much work!" she exclaimed, shaking her head. "I don't have time for that!" Perhaps it was the day...stress, frustration? But I squinted a bit as I replied,

"Well, then you won't have great hair." Her mouth dropped a little as I turned and walked away.

I admit, I was a bit harsh that day, but I am shocked and dismayed at how many people I encounter in a week that seem caught in a sticky web of immobilized frustration. They're baffled that the world isn't working out quite the way they'd hoped - but in that same moment, don't know who to blame! And there, my friends, is the goop of the matter. For blame indeed, is a viscous thing. As you fling it about, it spatters the room and leaves you covered as much as your targets...rather maddening, really.

I've blamed. Lost years a ways back attempting to ferret out who was at fault for the left turn my life had taken. Alas, the quest ended with me standing in front of a mirror. The frame chipped, the glass cracked...but truth is truth. The choices had been mine. There were other actors on that stage, but I was there as well. If I wanted something different, something greater - it was up to me. In that sentence, in accepting that reality, thus enters the magic - *effort*.

The aspiration, the application, the battle. The discipline, intention and push. Resolution, struggle...and triumph. They are all *ours*. It's in the *effort* where we discover how strong we are. Our capability, our cleverness, and our power. Within each of us is a life to be *lived*. Not endured or tolerated, we were meant for more than that!

Dreams, desires and goals + *effort* = success, fulfillment and joy.

Dreams, desires and goals + more dreams = wishes. And if wishes were fishes, we'd walk upon the sea. *(thank you, mum, for that one)*

Dreams, desires and goals + whining & complaining = will likely cost you the relationship you have with anyone who actually is on the road to success, fulfillment and joy.

I have one thing I tell anyone who is "always late" or "doesn't have enough time" to get something done. **Watch less TV and get up earlier.** Period. Our nation is in the midst of an epidemic of lethargy. Yes, you can see it in our physical health - but it's also there in our divorce rates, our juvenile centers, and our alcohol consumption. I feel like we have taken what is supposed to be simple, and crammed a zillion other things into that equation. All of the "what ifs" and "buts" that we can imagine; excuses and reasons for our lack of success - when the monster in the room is seated dead center in the rejection of our own potential.

YOU were meant to be amazing. *But amazing doesn't happen by accident!* It doesn't fall from the sky and rarely mails itself to your door. Opportunity may do that - but then, the amazing part is in your hands. In mine.

You want a deeper marriage? A better sex life? Respectful kids and an obedient dog, a cleaner house? Great hair?? Then research, come up with a plan, and *begin.*

My dreams are certainly different than many, the content isn't ever up for debate. *(I once met a woman whose heart's desire it was to dye her hair purple and ride elephants - I smile every time I think of her and hope she is a lovely shade of violet)* Wrapping your mind, your time, and your muscles around the reality that is the dream? That is the beginning.

And the beginning is within your grasp.

Blinds and Leaves and Curtains of the Soul

Spring has come to my world. I crave it. The rattle of barren branches in the large trees behind us begins to soften as tender buds blur the stark lines. I mourn a little in the fall as the leaves that shroud my private world drop to expose my kitchen window to curious eyes. Daily now, the slow creep of green blots out more and more of the sky, hides the neighbor's fences, the red doghouse within their yard. Thank goodness for this blessing as with the increase of temperature, so the decrease in layers of my clothing. Come the humid heat of July and in this ancient assemblage of rafters and lathe that boasts of no air conditioning - I shall near be naked. Such is summer.

I love the windows here. Huge. They usher in the golden light of morning with arms outstretched, coax the rain-scented breeze to enter, frame the stars like brilliant works of art. Decrepit, they are. Older than my children and likely me, they haven't sealed tight in a decade and clatter a bit when the wind is particularly determined. The wavy glass would make most replace them, but I rather like the muted kaleidoscope of color they contain.

I have sheers on all but the front ones. Heavy drapes seem to drag at me, I've never been able to bear them. I need the light, to see the world I'm in. I know that means that in the dark of night with illumination inside, I may be seen. Ah well, the price I pay for sunshine spilled across the walls. Sometimes I drive past our old apartment, the first floor of a monumental Victorian home, complete with glass sunroom (*my previous studio)* and eight foot tall cherry pillars that encase a fireplace I believed to only exist in magazines. The crushing thing is now, whatever current tenant abides there, they've chosen to brick in the lovely windows with blinds twisted tight, walling off sun and air. Sealing away the glory of the magnolia tree just outside the kitchen, the azaleas across the way. Every single window is like some clouded cataract of a blind eye. Staring and seeing nothing. Even the sunroom is cloaked in silent opaque panels. How do you breathe in rooms devoid of sky and earth?

The everlasting quest for privacy. It's funny as we track our celebrities and investigate our politicians, we've come to accept some invasions of privacy. The recent cellphone hacking has left the bitter tang of blood in our mouths; while in the same moment I cannot help amazement at the mass of tweeted daily minutia, revealing so much about private worlds. Who had lunch with who, where...and damn, I even know what salad dressing they like! We seem to publish ourselves quite boldly in the virtual world. I wonder how much of this is true disclosure versus mediocre distraction. Or worse, delusion. As if 200 people knowing what you had for lunch means you're not about to lose your job...the house...the marriage.

I wonder if privacy helps with pain. Or compounds it. I am very reserved about discussing things that hurt me. Most of the time simply because I love the hurter. Despite all. Isn't that the case so often? The ones we love the deepest, they wield the sharpest knives. Spouses berating each other, children railing at parents, coworker rants, how do they not consider that these previously private matters in our society - privacy which allowed for healing and moving on - once made public, are like acid? They eat away at the very fabric of life, the sustaining parts. While it may feel grand to have eighty 'likes' and "attaboys" in the moment, when the storm has passed, you're still there. Your school chum three states away is just buying laundry soap and eggs and has utterly forgotten your situation. But your partner hasn't. And yet...as the tears silently slip down my cheeks, the darkness the only witness, is this better? We're supposed to be wiser with age, more together. I'm not sure I believe that anymore.

    Spring is here. I'm so glad the honeysuckle is stealing up the tree outside the dining room. Wrapping tendrils of ivy love about the trunk, spilling delicious blooms into the corner of my world. Soon I won't be able to see the porch next door. And they not me. If I want to sip whiskey and weep till dawn, I can. Privately.

Freckles and Wrinkles and Markings of the Soul

The sun has arrived. June, her arms filled with a bounty of flowers and flush with the scent of summer, waits just beyond the door. The magical promise of fire flies glinting in her eyes, long days and even longer nights languid with music and laughter and smoke from the bonfire. Oh, my heart stirs!

My grandmother, passing ninety-five some time ago, has come to stay for a spell. Her name is Elva. A proper sort of name for almost five feet of southern charm. My days are slower now, a mingling of school year's end rush and the shuffle of elderly footsteps. She makes me pause, abandon projects and lists for lazy afternoons of stories and cold limeade on an herb lined porch. The speakers hidden beneath the old oak table filling the air with Nina Simone and Martin Sexton, music to remember by. Worlds lost, revisited.

I spend my mornings in love with dirt, coaxing tiny leaves from the earth. Pruning and cutting and edging our world; the sun's touch warm on my skin. An igneous heat that permeates my flesh, filtering down beneath the surface of sinew and bone to whisper to my soul...."*Awake.*"

I pause in the hall before the mirror. Her flushed cheeks and tangled hair surprise me. Somehow the unkempt wild version of me seems younger. Bare skin damp with exertion, white shadows beneath spaghetti straps vivid against tan speckled shoulders that trumpet the success of weeded tomatoes and basil thriving. Summer's blush, this is. Gram calls.

Icy tumblers leave wet rings on the blue and green bits of glass, a mosaic reminder of how beautiful broken can be. Her hand trembles as she sips, the act taking her full attention, brow furrowed. Libations safely returned to the table, she tilts her head, white hair tossed softly in the breeze. "Have I told you about the first time I saw Ed? That crazy Cates boy...."

The satin webs that frame her eyes, creases etched by a thousand smiles, a thousand tears....joy and anger and sorrow. A life carved into the flesh of a woman, two husbands and three sons buried. How cruel the hand of Fate can be. But here, in her granddaughter's home, three rowdy great grandsons atumble, rosemary studded beef saturating the air as it slowly roasts inside, the day unhurried and smelling of fresh-cut grass. Telling tales to this freckled woman masquerading as a girl. Lord, thank you for the opportunity to pour out...and to take in. Freckles and wrinkles and markings of the soul.

Roots

Last spring, we planted a tree in our front yard. In time it will add a smidgen of privacy to the porch we spend long hours upon, and who doesn't love cruising down a tree-lined avenue? While it was indeed the wrong time of year to move a tree, we forged ahead. If you plant in the fall, the tree is settled and then can rest and acclimate to new ground. When you do it in the spring, it's plunked down and immediately the world demands, "Blossoms, leaves and fruit!"

I was so proud the evening we dug out the circle in our lawn, knelt to insert the burlap wrapped ball into the ground, tenderly cut the string holding it all together. I remember the way the dirt felt under my nails as we pushed it in to surround the roots with dark loamy love. We began the summer of watering - and hoping.

I called my mum to ask about a stake. Everywhere I looked were little trees guarded by tall rigid planks of wood thrust deep into the ground. Each twiggy trunk was tied to their guards; braided cord promising safety in the storm while still seeming a bit strangulating at the same time. My mother is a horticulturist with a green *arm*, I seriously suspect she can make stones grow. I was slightly taken aback when she vehemently told me,

"No, the stakes make the trees weak." What? I thought they were to protect the baby trees, keep them from falling in a wind. But as I listened, her words rang true...in so many ways. You see, the most important part of a tree's job upon transplant, is to grow roots. Deeply. That neat and tidy ball that you carry home from the nursery is like the fat end of a weeble wobble and it must plunge its fibrous fingers down into the earth, entwining themselves in the world beneath lest it simply be blown over when the storms arrive.

But do you know what makes the roots grow? Being shaken. Every breeze, every thunderstorm, as the tree is rattled, it reaches deeper. The only way our sapling would make it through the treacherous years ahead, was for us to let it tremble through the gusts and gales of summer, shudder through winter's grip. Yes, there is risk - for once in a while a tempest may snap a trunk...but very rarely.

And so we watered and hoped. The August heat arrived and we watered more. The leaves dropped one by one as if plucked by October's frosty claws, and while the winter has been mild, snow draped the barren branches a time or two. I'm rather amazed that the simplest things in life truly do provide intense, innocent joy. The buds that swelled on twiggy tips were sheer delight. This early warmth burst them open the same day the robins returned to argue with the squirrels over the neighbor's feeder. Spring has arrived!

I've spent many days on my porch, fingers wrapped around coffee or whiskey, contemplating that tree. Good days...and hard ones. While the leaves were filling out, one of my boys broke a leg. As the branches stretched in glory to the sky, my husband had a seizure and lost the ability to drive. The tempests of life do surprise us sometimes; shocking how they can arrive in a moment wreaking havoc, and then be gone. At times the devastation is minor, others it redefines the color of the sky. But every cloudburst and squall - they're making us strong enough to face the hurricane. When jobs evaporate and cars crash and children wander in treacherous lands...when money is scarce and plans disintegrate and the future is suddenly unknown. When your heart aches and tears trace the curve of your cheeks....can you feel it?

You're growing roots.

Summer

I almost wish we were butterflies and liv'd but three summer days - three such days with you I could fill with more delight than fifty common years could ever contain.
John Keats

Fireflies

The sky seems like a watercolor love story. Blue and crimson dancing in each other's arms, their passion spilling over the horizon in a tangle of violet and tangerine ecstasy. Alana Davis whispers in my ear and the breeze brings murmurs of rosemary and sweet basil as it meanders through the potted herbs on the porch rail. Evening has come, shrouding our neighborhood in her velvet cloak of hush. She stills the pulse, blurs the parameters of the day.

There, beyond the fence, the flash that causes my heart to skip. Memories...

Raised on that Colorado farm, half of a mountain 9,000 feet above sea level, was a life...apart. Isolation incarnate. No television, no neighbors, three hundred animals and eighty acres and more than my share of loneliness, I fear. This was battled (*as often is*) by the magic of the literary world - adventure and fantasy became my addictions of choice. I flew through the heavens on gauzy wings that swept me from the reality of mucking pens and milking goats. *(while I am forever grateful for my upbringing now, what child relishes such things?)* Fast forward years and the farm was sold, my mother's health required a lower elevation; Dad had found something suitable, and we trekked across the country in a whirlwind of possibility to the level lands of Maryland. I was terrified.

Society awaited. Cars and teenagers and excitement unleashed. A long journey, exhaustion, and the first night <u>There</u>. A "there" with no horses, no chickens...and no sleep. I wandered the unfamiliar carpeted halls, the rooms dimly lit by streetlights beyond curtained glass - something that stopped me in my tracks in and of itself. Streetlights? Total foreign currency.

A glass of water, sipped in a stranger's kitchen filled with ghosts unknown. The silk of my nightgown chilly - air-conditioning, another exotic. And there, standing at the kitchen sink, my gaze was captured by the flickers of light that glimmered in the mist over the pond at the end of the yard. An incandescent dance that swirled beneath the stars.

We had fairies! What other conclusion was there?? My heart pounding as if to burst from my chest, the glass abandoned on the counter, I stumbled down the stairs to the back door and out into the damp June night. It was magic, that moment. Still, my heart remembers the joy as I chased the lights down the long hill, the grass wet beneath my bare feet, my hair streaming behind me in the thick humid air.

Fireflies. I'd never seen them before. I stayed for hours, catching them to watch them crawl along my fingers and leap into the air again and again; my fascination as if I were four, rather than fourteen. I think I fell in love with the east coast that night. Alone, damp and giggling in the dark of a summer's night as the magic of my dreams invaded my waking world.

Happy summer, my friends.

Summer Rain

A quarter to eight found me with feet tucked up, curled into a chair on the porch. An indian print shawl of gold and black and umber draped over a chocolate sundress that smelled faintly of the fajitas and saffron rice of dinner. A glass of wine upon the table beside me; a novel, pages slightly tacky in the humid air, resting in my lap. Suddenly the dark clouds that have scuttled across the sky all afternoon broke in the evening breeze, golden light burst through the air - June's last stand on a day decidedly resembling April. And it began to rain.

Oh, the splendor that is sunlit rain! Were that I had such a camera to capture the jewel-like waterfall that cascaded from the heavens, as if Mother Nature had held her aqueous breath all day and then let it out in a glorious deluge of glittering waves. It seemed the world paused. The leaves of the dogwood danced in tune with the giant oak across the way; the herbs along the rails shimmied, their essence painting the air with the scent of green and warmth and delicious promise. Paper pages of lust and love and death forgotten under damp kisses on my cheeks and soft wet trails across my shoulder, the seduction of summer.

The rain has passed now, the sunlight faded into the grey that announces the arrival of eve. The patter of drips along the porch rail are a piano that plays along with my thoughts...

Home....and Soul Improvement

Sometimes when you least expect it, the air gets let out of the room. Like someone leached the color from the sun and knocked you to the floor. I'm left gasping and wondering how dark the bruises on my knees will be from the landing. Life isn't fair. It isn't even polite about it. How we handle these times...how we grab the rail and drag ourselves up, frayed robe soaking in the tears. Heave a shuddered breath. And then another. How we do this, is the ink of us...writing our story.

I work. Utterly cliché, I realize this; but when the world has fallen off its axis, this is how I cope. My emotional realm is a minefield somehow tacked together with spider webbing, treacherously fragile and perilous to enter. And thus, in the name of self-preservation, I pick up a hammer. Lug the ladder to the second floor. Gallons of paint and three trips to Home Depot later, the bedroom has been refinished. Stenciling added, wrought iron hung, the fireplace in it given a face lift. Exhaustion temporarily erases memories.

The next day it begins again. Only now in my studio. Rip apart the desk and a hundred times down the stairs it seems, to haul its broken pieces to the curb. Halfway through I realize I have streaks of dust and grime smeared across my dampened cheeks. I scrape at them angrily with the rag I used to wipe the sink, adding green paint to the mess. Everything is a mess.

I don't answer the phone. I know that I push everyone as far away as I can, hiding the ache. I run from friends, family...even strangers. I hide behind closed doors and glib comments. Texts that end in "lol." I press an ice-pack to my swollen eyes before the boys come through the door. Again. Wash my hands and put cookies on a plate for them to have with homework. Cookies can distract anyone.

I find myself wondering as I spend hour upon hour working on my physical world; sweat and blood, blisters and a missing knuckle...do I somehow think this is going to mend the other? Is this the result of too many hours of home improvement television? Do we really believe that a new kitchen can restore a marriage? A backyard makeover can rebuild a relationship? The home improvement movement has hit a jackpot of staggering proportions. It seems rather delusional. But then again, a delusion or two, or just a distraction to keep from thinking...could be worse. Sometimes simply moving, moving at all, keeps us from the edge.

I don't know how anyone else does this - gets through. My rational mind tells me there is another side to get to, waiting. My emotional one doubts. In the meantime, I've ripped off two nails and scraped the skin from my knee.

But the studio looks great.

The Murder of Quiet

Driving home from the market today, I sat at an intersection next to a mini-van with children in it. Certainly not that remarkable, I assure you, however, there were also tv screens. *Three of them.* Attached to the back of the seats in front, all three had a different program on and three little heads had three sets of earbuds and while mom was chatting to whomever on her blue tooth, there was an air of....what? Peace? Not exactly. Isolation? Detachment?

Flashbacks of my childhood grocery days - my sisters and I rattling on, joking, laughing. *(to the point that my mother actually used to PAY us a quarter if we could be quiet the whole way home)* But none the less, there was a curious satisfying mingling; ideas and thoughts and life. Family.

I turned the corner and headed home. Parking, I noticed the neighbor cutting his lawn, i-pod attached. A couple walked by, pushing a stroller with a toddler - she was on her cell phone, he was messing with a black berry and the toddler? Had some kind of hand-held game that was maniacally beeping and buzzing to his obvious delight. I walked inside the house, dropping keys on the entry table. Kicking my shoes under the bench I made my way to the kitchen with my culinary loot. The window was open, a breeze tickled the back of my neck as I slid the onions into their basket, nestled peaches and plums together in the bowl, packed away the eggs and cheese and milk. I could hear the birds in the backyard. A distant dog barking. Leaning against the counter, I just closed my eyes and smiled. You know that feeling? So *good* to be home.

Dinner begun, slicing bacon and onions, the sizzle in the pan, delicious aromas filled the room and I thought about my day. What I'd said, whom I met...and it suddenly occurred to me, *I wonder if that couple thinks - through the noise?* The incessant blur that is our technological revolution. It's a barrage. An attack on the senses and the mind as we rise each day. The "convenience" we demand: portable everything. Music everywhere we go, cell phones and crackberries and games - oh, the holiest of grails: *entertainment.* Heaven forbid you actually might have to wait in line at the post office without having a *game* to play. And I wonder, could we design a study, concoct a thesis, could there really be a correlation between the moral disintegration of our society, the eroding of our families...and the simple lack of quiet?

In the quiet, there is only you. In the quiet, there your actions are to be faced. Decisions made in haste are rethought. Apologies composed as you hear your own angry words reverberating inside your mind. In the quiet, goals are set. Dreams are discovered, plans made, ideas go from mere wisps to full-fledged intentions. The quiet is not always comfortable. It holds ghosts, mistakes. But it is within this *very discomfort* that we surpass the animal world - where our humanity thrives, where we become...*more.*

There was a time, when going for a walk meant thinking about your day, not sifting through the latest playlist. When we mowed our lawns or planted our gardens, we examined our lives. Have we lost this in the endless quest for entertainment and distraction? Can we not ride the bus and actually have a pleasant conversation with a stranger? Must we all be surrounded by a wall, a distance created by cords and headphones?

Are we "entertaining" ourselves into isolation? And within this individual plastic creation, are we becoming so self-centered, so absolutely *used* to having it "our way," that the slightest detour from this - the inconvenience of another's schedule, wishes, *taste in music* for goodness sakes, becomes an intrusion?

Some of the greatest moments of my life, the beginnings of glorious love and friendships and joy, were inconveniences and interruptions. The greatest epiphanies in my heart - both blissful and agonizing - occurred in the quiet. Today, tonight, on your commute, on your walk, turn off the noise. Unplug. Just listen. Listen to your heart, the voice of your soul.

You may be wonderfully surprised by what it has to say.

Healthy

It's funny, Websters defines healthy as: *possessing or enjoying good health or a sound and vigorous mentality*. And yet I'm beginning to truly believe that your level of "healthiness" is just a direct and somewhat backwards reflection of your level of self-deception. I seem to be surrounded by people who are "making healthier choices" while they wallow in pits of blackened tar. One friend brags that she spent an hour at the gym working out - and during our 20 minute dialog over the phone, she consumed an entire pint of Cherry Garcia. Another is discovering "Buddhist peace" while continuing to drown in the suffocating relationship she swears completes her. A fellow artist I know has taken up jogging...because he passes Mrs. Felp's house; and she offers refreshment of a most *personal* nature. His wife is thrilled with his new interest in getting healthy.

Life is a maze. We navigate with a slew of handicaps to challenge us. While one might be blind, another has no arms, one limps, one crawls. One has money, another none. Education, experience, hell - just good taste and manners can either put you ahead, or if you are lacking them, behind. So we traverse. Questing after a healthy life; after all, health is the "key" to happiness, right? It matters not the magnitude of financial or relational wealth you possess if you don't have your health! Our media dishes out laugh-track laden shows that portray deception, ridicule, and exploitation as amusing. Our evening viewing is peppered with advertisements for new medications that have such gruesome side effects as to make one wonder who in the blazes would actually take them. Our salad bars are dripping with thousand calorie dressings, crunchies and toppings which eradicate all validity of wellness from the copious plates being carted by smiling people secretly confused as to why they cannot drop those pounds since they are working *so hard* to eat healthy.

Exercise, religion, food - has it all become one spiritual quest? I suppose it might be; but what are we seeking? Excitement? Satisfaction? Distraction? Perhaps "balance" is the only real healthy. As each of us indulges our vices, do we make up for it somewhere else? Like benevolent vampires. I wish I knew the weight of it all - does a thriving career balance out a disintegrating marriage? Does giving up a career to stay home with the children counteract slim Christmases and canceled vacations? Is being slender worth skipping cheese? *(dear GOD, please say no!)* Where is the handbook that has the calculated mass of everything? Can someone please write one?? My personal system is called "what would you pay."

My darling friend used to color her hair. And she cut coupons. Buying what was on sale plus a coupon might save her 3 or 4 bucks! However, the results at times did not resemble those gorgeous Feria commercials. There are actually shades of red that should be labeled "Whore in the Store" and "Crispy Deep Fried Rouge." One Sunday I asked her, "Love...your hair looks like...well, if I had a magic wand, would you pay me $3 to fix your hair before you go to church?" She looked at me and then laughed. She swore she'd never use another coupon. What would you pay to have it turn out JUST right? When you have that horrid migraine, would you pay someone the $15 you'd save going to the drugstore, the cheap grocery, AND the discount market for everything on your list? That particular day, at that *particular* time - just pay the extra $15 and get it all at one place. Is it worth doing laundry at midnight to spend the afternoon playing scrabble on the front porch? Cutting the lawn in the rain so you don't miss the game? Skip the ice-cream so you can have the brie? What would you pay?

    Does sacrifice for iniquity equal healthy? I'm just like everyone else. I justify, I explain, I rationalize my decisions. I seek to balance my hunger for the nefarious with bean sprouts. Twenty minutes ago I put Splenda with fiber in my whiskey.

I Am Not

I recently heard the story of a woman who had been burned. The kind of horror that would normally end in death; it was past disfiguring. beyond ghastly. In fact, it had left ghastly somewhere in another state and drove on for days. She had lost her face.

Now this was actually a tale of victory. The strength of the human soul is astounding. I find myself in mesmerized awe of people like this - beings that seem to have hearts made of an interminable flame; they never stop, never relinquish, never surrender. I have faith that we are not given what we cannot handle; though in the moment, this may be a bare thread I cling to, a rope frayed and unraveled. There have indeed been days of anguish when I have whispered to myself, "today is just tomorrow's yesterday" over and over in order to survive. But survive, I did.

This woman, she did more than survive. She *conquered.* She rode side by side with Death and then laughed at his amateur antics. She was astounding. She was magnificent. She was beautiful - *in every sense of that word* - which floored me. We all know how a person's "inside" effects how we see or feel about them. Remember that really handsome fellow that made your heart pound - until you heard him berate the waitress and make fun of the guy in glasses? Suddenly he wasn't so handsome. Or that woman with the body of a Greek goddess...who turned out to have the mouth of a sailor and the mind of a Dynasty gold-digger? (*Run, Forest, ruuuun!*) Life seems often a play; we choose costumes, but the soul is eternal.

They had rebuilt her face. They tried so hard. Doctors with

kind hands and kinder hearts had spent hundreds of hours researching and planning, removing skin here to put it there. Sewing and tucking, attempting the impossible. So calm, she sat there. Twisted scar tissue where lips should be.

"It took me two years to learn that I am not my body." Immeasurable, shattering truth. I have lain awake for hours, this running like a movie looped, in my mind. Her face, her body, the agony represented there that has taken years to overcome, entire *months* lived floating in a saline tank. She radiated peace as if she were the sun. She was the embodiment of light and joy and serenity. She was beautiful.

I feel the entire meaning of life might be summed up in that one sentence. We live trapped within the flesh granted us and spend decades adjusting it. Shifting it to arrange the fit; painting and dyeing and cloaking it. All the while, we are granted opportunity after opportunity to learn the futility of this. We judge and assess and classify - on something as substantial as the wind. So mortal, so temporary. You are not your flesh.

I tell my students, (*I've taken on a college English class from time to time*) that they <u>must</u> write. That all that is their soul, what they have ever felt or thought will be lost forever when they die, if they do not. That everything they've done and discovered and learned will not matter if they do not write. That they will eventually be forgotten, if they do not write.

Letters and words are the landscape of the soul. It is here that I am seen, unencumbered. My children have my face etched upon their hearts....but you do not. You don't know the freckles on my nose or the tattoo on my ankle or the length of my auburn hair. For really, it does not matter, flesh so corporeal. As I type this, I wonder how my life would change, should I lose my face. Every physical interaction would be altered. From the market to the bank to my marriage. Neighbors and strangers in passing cars. They would stare, survey, appraise me. But not here. Here you and I would still meet, linger...share. For here is it only the soul.

    I am not my body.

The Wettest Car. Ever.

Is "wettest" a word? Like "completely soaked to the point of saturation in the absolutest sense." *(yeah, I know - sue me for "absolutest")* So I used to drive a Cadillac. Ooooh...you know those hot commercials with the rockin' babe in skimpy attire that make you wonder if you're going to the store or about to orgasm? *(usually there is a tunnel, flashing lights, and glimpses of gleaming metal and a stiletto heeled, perfectly manicured sexy foot pressing the...uh....gas pedal....hang on, gimme a minute....whew)* Um, you can scratch those. Now, I *have* actually had complete strangers stop me and offer me a check for my car - no kidding. My gleaming, gorgeous, two door, low rider, SOLID GOLD pimp-me-like-you-mean-it Cadillac. Yes, the bank SECURITY GUARD actually personally ushers me in the lot and comes to check my tires. He's like, "you know, you got a paint chip on the bumper?" I'm like, "Man, it's a 1990 - she's sweet." HA!

HOWEVER. There was an expiration date. Didn't they tell you? Your car has one too. It's usually on a really important day. Like your wedding day...or the day you're leaving for vacation. Maybe it's the day you have two dentist appointments *(doesn't everyone do this? dammit, get it OUT of the way!)*, a lunch with a long lost pal *(ok, so I drank a shake, stupid novocaine),* and a job interview. *(pass off the shake stain you drooled as hand lotion)* THAT is the day your car expires.

In two days' time, it was over. The right blinker quit working. The breaks began SCREAMING - not squealing like a forked pig - this pig got run over and then they *backed up*. The driver's seatbelt developed a completely unpredictable ability to unlatch by itself, usually when you're doing about 65mph. The "gleaming metal" on the outside of the passenger's door came loose; it flapped in the wind like a dying crow until your teeth rattled. The caddie has an awesome air conditioner...the fan stopped. The fan is located somehow behind the *entire* engine. As in "cash-in-the-kids-college-fund" money just to GET to it, much less replace it. It makes deliciously cold air - that you can feel dribbling over your toes if you do about 70mph. The dash lights went out.

    The locks would randomly engage. Especially when you were unloading groceries. The windows...well, apparently there are these plastic clips; they ride in the track up and down inside of the door, attaching them to the gizmo that makes the windows do their thing. They broke. The windows are either up - or if you try to roll them down, they crash with a heart-stopping thunk into the bottom of the door never to be seen again unless you cram your fingers into the slot and physically hoist them up again; a feat only my 6'4" husband has been able to achieve. So the windows are either UP - it's 91* in that lovely August summer in the 'Burg and you redefine "roast;" or the windows are DOWN. Unable to be rolled up until my dear man comes home from work.

    There I was, on a broiling humid Monday evening - headed to pick up the boys from my ex's, and it began to rain. *Ahem* Make that, *"Dear GOD I am NOT NOAH and I don't have an ARC!!"* kinda rain. And <u>everyone</u> is staring. There is enough water coming down from the sky to drown a small army of zebras and both of my very LARGE windows, basically the length of the car, are completely down. Torrents of rain are soaking me, my hair is plastered to my head, glasses fogged, cars hitting "puddles" are sending oceanic waves across my shoulders....

So I went with it. What the hell else could I do? Found some hard core Rage Against the Machine and turned it WAAAY up. I whipped my hair up into a soggy mess on top of my head with pieces curling in the wind, black spaghetti tank straps falling off my shoulders as the mascara smeared across my cheeks. I was HOT. I was "I don't care about your cozy vanilla-scented minivan with your mocha chino and booster seats! I am WET and WILD and ROCKIN'!"

The boys were flabbergasted. They were ecstatic. They whooped and hollered the whole way home. I told them they wouldn't have to take showers. Loved that caddie.

Enough

The sun drags golden fingers across the sky, chasing the dregs of night away. Green eyes meet their twin in the silver framed reflection, careless and distracted with the mental list accumulating even as the coffee brews. Pushing my hair back, icy water sluices across my cheeks, dripping down my neck to shimmer on the ridges and valleys of my clavicle. Morning.

Stare to stare…no make-up, no pretense. Strange this person I am more intimate with than any other. I'm not entirely certain she likes me at times. Bare feet slap on cool floors, the vacuum smack of the fridge as heavy cream paints whirls of beige into the mahogany elixir that whispers my name. Daylight.

I face her again, reaching for pencil and powder, rouge and the glide of lip stain. And I pause. Honesty. There was a day, years and years ago - a photographer young and eager, wishing to please as well as to sell.

"Do you want me to hide them?" she asked, snapping her gum as she tilted her head.

"Hide what?" Perplexed.

"Those…" She pointed. And to a mirror I turned. Like my mother's, they are. *(a face beloved, memorized, cherished)* One on the side of my nose, the other nearly hidden in the curve beneath my lower lip. Flaws.

A blemish of no color, a flesh-toned mole. Soft mounds that lay quietly, announcing that I wasn't made in a mold. Wasn't carved for display. Noticed when one is within the realm of intimacy, or digital photography. I've spent years coming to terms with their firm hold upon my profile. Was advised to knife them off in high school, teased by family and schoolmates. Witches have such knobs...so I've been told.

Strange the journey from insecurity and craving elusive perfection through the acceptance of the immutable to embracing the unique. I fear much of this journey I have mapped out in my mind, highlighting the path and pledging my heart to following it. However, it's possible I may be a bit stuck in that middle area. What we see in the mirror is as slanted as a funhouse; the shortcomings exaggerated, defects looming larger than life, voices from the past echoing long beyond their deserved graves.

I know each of us carry our ghosts. We size up and compare, lining up imperfections and insults, rating them on some personal scale as if in classifying them on the lower end, they might be diminished. The immensity of a history is only known by the self. For, try as we might to communicate such an experience, there was only one soul that lived your particular story. One heart that laughed and bled that night when the stars seemed brighter than the sun.

The world can be cruel. Perfection is a lost cause, I've learned, joyfully so. *(well, with the exception of a good hollandaise sauce or a sunset)* Parenthood is a bog of quicksand and contemplation; relationships a braid of sacrifice, laughter, and forgiveness; and self-love an exercise in repetition and listening: I am good. I am unique. I am enough.

Records

    The air is that delicious shade of amber when night hovers just beyond daylight's reach. The cool of the eve is wondrous after the scorch and scrape of August sun. Somewhere between a siren's call and the battle anthem of summer, the cicadas song echoes through the trees, reverberating in my mind as memories of previous summers flit and dart like a movie reel spliced. That sound accompanied my first kiss. My first heartbreak. There was the smell of funnel cakes and carnival lights and breathless anticipation...

    Tonight I sat on the front porch with my grandmother. She's visiting for a few weeks, enjoying the great grandsons while the weather is warm. Ninety-six years she has walked the earth...yet so small. Almost some strange humor as my six foot frame curls into the twin of the chair she seems childlike in, not even five feet tall. She's wearing long johns beneath her clothes; a bizarre and slightly odd commentary on the fragile straps of the gauzy sundress that barely makes me presentable in this humid heat. How age changes things.

    The light in her eyes is fierce, strong as her mind repeats the loops it has grown accustomed to. I believe the passionate moments - be them lovely or terrible - carve the deepest grooves in the records that play as we age. I wonder, as she tells me again of meeting my grandfather, my eyes tracing the lines that web her cheeks, the curve of her ear...I wonder who I will be, what records I'll play. For her, a widow with three young sons before she was even twenty, one of the records she plays was being desired by my grandfather despite the hungry mouths she brought along, "that wild Cates boy." His fast car swept her away, and his monthly check when he was gone in the service kept her afloat along with family. So much tragedy, so much hunger. Starvation for food, love, security...a time in history we, so blessed, will never truly understand.

  And now, so small, so weak, she tells me how the men still want her. I smile. I even smile with a wink and a chuckle and she grins back. She shifts in her chair, pulls at the sleeve of her long underwear, and shakes her head softly. She reaches out to stroke Hazel's back and asks when my husband, whose name she often forgets, will be home. Sometimes her persistence that "someone is out there" or that "he was looking at me" can be frustrating, life is demanding enough without adding in constant reassurances and appeasements. But I've begun to think that she clings to this idea because to fully admit that no one really "wants" her anymore, would be to somehow lose meaning, purpose. She wrestles with being a burden - yet in the same scrappy moment, I think she thoroughly enjoys the 'hand and foot treatment' she receives. She knows it not, but in a world of fragmented families, to be tucked in bed with a kiss, and have breakfast laid out each morning…I can only pray I am loved and cared for one day, as she.

  It's difficult at times, being stuck in the timewarp she resides within. My parents are stunning in the years of care - years of bacon and eggs, duplicate loads of laundry, 'please-don't-touch-that' and cleaning up the spills. The privacy they've sacrificed is beyond calculation - I fear at times my mum hedges on the edge of sainthood. This level of care isn't easy, but I enjoy the opportunities I have to give my parents respite as well as challenge my own family to the joy and discovery that it is to live with an elder. Lessons in patience, movement on shuffle, hours of quiet.

    The crickets have struck up their serenade and the streetlights are glowing softly. She's begun to repeat herself, in that record-skip way she does, as I lead her inside for the night. I wonder what my records will be....

On Waiting

Inside of the dash and scramble, the glory and anguish, the blaze and murk of gloom - within this story we are writing as we breathe and love and hate and dream, are moments that define us. Much as ink on parchment.

The rasp of my charcoal seems loud in the room as I sketch the arch of the brow. Black dust drifts across her cheek, I blow it away. Bars of afternoon sunshine trace lazy patterns on the floor, shifting as the curtains billow in the breeze of the open window. I am waiting.

Waiting is a hiatus. A pause. A breath held. I find few things tell me more about a person than watching them wait. The ability to wait with elegance is a component I believe supremely important to a complete childhood upbringing; it's the foundation of civilized life as we know it. Waiting to speak, play, ask. Stand in line, raise your hand, take your turn. Waiting, if carefully nurtured, gives birth to anticipation; delicious appreciation of the moment achieved. However, if not practiced regularly with self-control and discipline, it can spawn rage, frustration, and an acidic impatience rooted in self-centeredness that will slowly eat away at any joy you hope to hold.

For waiting is like the air. As the seasons and the sun and death and summer rain - waiting is inevitable. From the moment of conception, we wait. For dawn, we wait. For dusk. For first kisses and true love and bended knee, we wait. For winter's end. The bread to rise, the light to turn, the children to sleep....we wait.

What do you do while you wait? My mother told me once, never to pray for patience. For such a prayer was the unleashing of disaster in your life; the upending of plans and goals, messes upon hold-ups upon delays - all which would, in the end, lead to patience. But a lesson of cost, be careful. I've never prayed thus, but still chuckle with friends about one day writing a book titled, "Living In The Two Percent." For by golly, if there is a 98% chance that all will work out just fine...I am in the two. Every. Time. And honestly, my closest friends laugh, cringe a little - and agree.

All is not lost, however, for within the hospital stays and duplicate paperwork and broken plans, I have found indeed almost a kinship with waiting. Perhaps it is that this world is endlessly fascinating to me. I can be mesmerized by the dust as it frolics on the wind and have spent an afternoon on my knees in the damp soil, taking pictures of the bleached skeleton of a tiny bird. The bones were like ivory threads, knit together with such artistry, such symmetry, their grace nearly took my breath away. Loveliness left in death's cold wake. I was waiting for the boys return from fishing that day; I never would have found those ossien beauties if I hadn't been stranded, time on my hands.

I've written some of my best work in the doctor's office. Composed poetry while in line at the bank. I carry pencils and charcoal in my purse, napkins and the back of old lists becoming my canvas when the waitress is lagging or the train late. I'm not claiming a passive acquiescence at all times, trust me - there is a storm abrew once in a while, but I find conquering my internal turmoil, my desire to demand and shout, to be strangely cathartic. Proof somehow, that

I may not be able to control the world - but I can control my response to it. The way we wait defines us, much as my chalk defines the shape of her eye, the curve of her cheek. Within this moment, I find time. Time I wouldn't have had to reflect, contemplate. Time to ruminate and wonder and muse.

    The art of the wait.

An Ocean

I've mentioned that in my early twenties, I spent several years living in Mexico, Guatemala, and some of the worst streets of Philadelphia. My first husband and I would act as 'house parents' and we'd be joined by 10-15 college kids for a few months at a time and get them connected and working with the orphanages, health clinics, and soup kitchens in the area. Amazing, the lives I saw changed. Hearts softened, souls healed. Sometimes there was joy so pure it felt like flying. Sometimes there was darkness so black it felt like the end of everything.

I dreamt the other night of Guatemala. While some of you may have vacationed in the lovely parts, there are villages still without electricity, towns full of families that scrape food out of the dust, children who have never seen a refrigerator. I learned so much when I was there. About myself, my fears, my expectations. I learned to long for toilets that flushed, craved brushing my teeth with tap water, sprayed the legs of my wood and rope cot with raid to keep the tarantulas from climbing into my blankets.

One day, we took a trip out to visit an orphanage that had asked us to come sing for them. Something so simple; our rag-tattered gang of off-key, couldn't-carry-a-tune-in-a-bucket, sunburned loons - and those children were ecstatic! They giggled and laughed and danced - it was a holiday, a treat, the best of presents. Such fun indeed…but the van was silent that night as we trundled back over dirt roads towards home; such simplicity and gratitude drapes a cloak of conviction over privileged shoulders.

Driving in another country is staggering. The fact that there are no car inspections, no rules, no lanes - insanity. Often cars run without operating lights, making night driving perilous. We almost didn't see them. The smashed little car, the larger one less so. There was a drunk man passed out in the dirt. And a sobbing, hysterical man in his 20's that came running towards us, his face streaked with tears and blood. His new bride was pinned in the car.

Our interpreter, Debbie, called for an ambulance, it was on the way. We were about ten minutes from the closest city. Meanwhile, the man I married the first time around was not good in emergencies and was slightly panicked. I left him in the van with the crew and asked them to pray. Debbie and I were nearly drug over to the smashed vehicle, the husband frantically gesturing at the car and pointing to his nose. Oh God, I could smell gas. We didn't have tools, but between us, we pried the door halfway open. Finally able to hold his wife's hand, he calmed down enough to tell us her name was Maria and his was Carlos. Headlights in the distance - the ambulance. I stood, waving my arms to get it to slow down. It was a pick-up truck with a piece of plywood in the back.

I was dumbfounded. Shocked into silence. This? This was the ambulance? The driver was efficient and soon produced a crow bar and wrenched the door the rest of the way open. Carlos seemed unable to let go of the unconscious Maria's hand so I found myself attempting to support her head and shoulders as we gingerly pulled her from the twisted wreck. Debbie had drug the plywood over and we carefully laid her down. There was so much blood. Maria's head was cradled in the palm of my hand and it shifted slightly as I knelt in the dirt....and then the tips of my fingers felt the bones of her skull move. Oh, God. In glare of the headlights I suddenly understood why Maria's head didn't look right. My heart nearly stopped. Debbie reached out as I inhaled sharply, drawing Carlos over to the other side of the board, sparing him the sight of his bride's broken body and his shattered dreams.

 We carried the board to the truck and slid it into the back, Carlos climbing up to sit next to her. I could hear him telling her he loved her over and over as he clutched her hand. I stood there, frozen, as the tail lights vanished down the dark road. Debbie had checked the drunk and said he was fine. He'd been tossed from his car when it t-boned theirs. Aside from some scrapes and bruises, he would be alright. She helped him to his car and then gently led me back to the van. I don't remember the rest of the ride home. I do remember getting into the shower with all my clothes on, watching Maria's blood wash down the drain, and sobbing till there was nothing left.

 I didn't have children then. Years later my boys would enter my life and I would understand a love that literally was cell and bone and sinew deep. Tomorrow is my fortieth birthday. I suppose it's only natural to find myself today sifting through what I am thankful for. Since that night, kneeling in the dark, I have never heard the wail of an ambulance and not closed my eyes for a moment, desperately grateful to live in a place where such a sound is only a phone call away. That my children live here. This gratitude is nearly overwhelming, immeasurable. It's an ocean.

Chosen Fragility

It was dusk. That magic that happens when the air seems to shimmer and glow as if Mother Nature were letting out her breath. The day's heat slowly bleeds away; the trees becoming silhouettes, black statues against a tangerine sky. Somewhere in the distance I could hear dogs barking and the laughter of children. Summer alchemy. That perfect blend of elements that seduces the eye to visit for a time.

Our front porch roof is rimmed with white fairy globes. Their gentle drape illuminates the hanging ivy and hummingbird feeder. Beneath are my potted herbs, rosemary and thyme and mint. A six foot tall avocado tree fills the corner next to the table I mosaicked last summer with blue and green glass, painstakingly broken by hand on a tattered kitchen towel while I knelt on the front walk. The antique playing board and chess set is to my right; my puppy, dear Hazel, at my feet.

I leave the lights on round the clock. Our home welcoming no matter if you're arriving for dinner or at midnight exhausted from the day; or awake before the dawn, sweet sleep forsaken you. I fear I dismiss the electric bill for peace of mind. Rather selfish of me, I suppose. What one is willing to pay for tranquility, hmmm?

It fluttered into view. On a crazy loop of a crashing flight, the moth fell heavily onto the back of my hand. I could feel the tiny feet clutching, a grip that might alarm if I wasn't so astonished. Its wing was damaged. The dust that grants their flight missing from nearly half the crooked appendage. It wobbled a bit, seeking better purchase on my flesh....and then lay still.

I don't know how long I sat there, my hand resting on the knee I had pulled up into my chair. The night settled herself slowly into the neighborhood. Softly she began to wrap the houses within my view in her cloak of quiet, nestling little heads to slumber beneath the stars. The moth, so fragile, still clinging to my warm skin, somehow seemed desperate, even in its unstirring perch. Though perhaps this was just me seeing myself.

Somehow for me, there is strength in anger. Even in the midst of betrayal and shock. Maybe it's because, though the storm is raging and the sky is black and I am forced to make decisions I never anticipated - I am still the one taking action. Though this may only be a desperate act of self-preservation, I choose.

Every relationship is a choice. Yes, emotions and feelings are grand, but we all know those days when it is simply putting one foot in front of the other, the plod of choice and commitment, rather than the merry twirl of flutters and desire. This is the day you get up with the flu and still make dinner...because the children must eat. When you haven't slept in 35 hours and you still go to work because the bills need paid. When words no longer have meaning, and actions are all that remain. Yes, somehow even in the stark trenches of choice, I find strength.

But then there is a moment...a pause. After you've chosen the plod - you've chosen to stay/try/commitment and vows and I *meant* them...regardless. Suddenly, after weeks, months of *choosing*...you realize the flutter has returned. With gossamer wings and delicate bones, that chrysalis of daily choice has metamorphasized into something else...become something more. Hope.

And in hope I am painfully, staggeringly, vulnerable. The winds of hope can lift you to the heavens...and smash you on the rocks leaving broken bits and shattered ends. Hope moves the choices to another's hands. Pries the power from your grasp leaving you staring at calloused empty palms. Hope paralyzes me.

The fireflies have settled in the trees, like God's Christmas lights out of season. I can smell the rain coming. I shift and with an ivory blur, the moth plunges out into the night. I hope it lands somewhere safe.

I hope.

Intimacy and Fear and Twinness

It's been an odd summer for me. Begun with such a visceral rampage of emotions, chasms so deep and dark, skies painted with the prism of fragile faith, paralyzing anguish and livid relief. I think, in a way, I overdosed on introspection. Facing some of my most unspoken fears forced an excavation of the soul; broken bits and lost bits and forgotten ones were found. In these moments, we discover much about ourselves. I curl in. Disengage. I'm not one to ask for help even on the best of days and this was so acutely displayed these last few months as to be painful to my friends and family. My sincerest apologies for this. Communication was impossible for me....hell, even the thoughts within my own skull were agony.

Recently I've watched in surprise as someone I know has gone through a similar season and yet, in complete juxtaposition of me, has publically announced every step of her journey; fears and hopes, updates and disappointments, all published via social media to hundreds, if not thousands, of people. I'm awed... amazed... terrified. That level of intimacy with so many is unthinkable for me. And yet a great deal of my life has been spent in a quest for intimacy; an attempt to fill a cavern so vast that held only shadows. Some might hazard this was a result of a rather isolated childhood and a family that I was never close to until ten years ago; but frankly the Why is so much less important than the Now. The Here is more relevant than the How. Forty years on this planet has taught me that one of our greatest mistakes is getting caught up, trapped within the Why and How, missing out on the gift of choice, forgiveness, and potential that is Now.

But it is true that my Now had a beginning. Everyone's does. In that quest for a soul mate I lunged toward the nearest hand offered - and thus the tragedy of my first marriage commenced. A man that would order me not to breathe on him, that didn't like touching. I was a fish thrashing about in a desiccated death valley of a relationship. Which brings me to the story of my second husband of six years now. His How is something that twists my soul every time I think of it. Oh, to be grateful for such heartache is a terrible thing...yet our Now is chiseled and sculpted by our Hows and Whys, is it not? This is his story, which has become my own…

Four and a half decades and our medicine has advanced in a miraculous way. But there was a day back then, when a young mother was told at eight and a half months pregnant, that her unborn baby had perished. There was no heartbeat to be found. She would have to carry the stillborn to term and endure labor while planning a funeral that included an eighteen inch coffin...she nearly shattered. Returning to the doctor, she insisted she could still feel movement and was assured this was merely a manifestation of her grief, and thus she wept and fragmented until the contractions began. Hours later a beautiful lifeless boy was born. And fifteen minutes after that, my husband Jason was also.

Can you imagine the sorrow and the joy of that moment? An excruciating combination that stained everyone in the room with the colors of despair and wonder. The world turned and life happened and Jason didn't discover he was a twin until he was fifteen years old. This suddenly explained his feelings of perpetual aloneness, an internal 'missing' that never ebbed, no matter the company. He dreamt, almost nightly, of sleeping wrapped around another, entwined. His first marriage also, was full of echoes and emptiness.

And then we found each other.

I know few who sleep as we do; a knot of limbs, flesh against flesh, where one ends and the other begins unknowable. His face on my neck, my lips against his arm, our breathing syncs and we slumber. Intimacy beyond my understanding at times.
Twins bound by life.

Heat

We hit 94* today. Molten lava, the sun was. Melting the clouds from the sky; searing the green from the dogwood leaves leaving crisp, curled brownness behind. Pouring coffee this morning, the warmth of the day teased me; its breath stirring the wisps of hair on my neck that had escaped the knot, whispering promises of fever.

Uncomfortable. Sticky. Complaints and wishes and visits to the pool. The eastern sun blazes and the day slowly boils. And yet...another heat.

3pm and walking to the kitchen I am aware of the silky slide of my thighs against one another. I fill my glass with ice cubes and take one more. Its frozen kiss almost burns as I run it across my lips, down my neck, across my bare shoulder. Shocking how quickly it melts, leaving dark trails dripping down the fabric of my dress.

Lovely, how such an unpleasant warmth leads to another, more delicious one. Damp skin and breathless lungs. I sit on steps of the porch, Hazel stretched out across the boards beside me. I shiver as the sweat tracing its way down my spine pools in the small curve at its base. And I wait, watching the horizon for his car…

We will eat with our fingers. After the sun has fled and the house has gone to sleep. We will drink from the same glass and I will lick the sauce from the edge of his lips. For it is summer...

May the world ignite.

Soul Ink

The tumult of summer storms has blown through, leaving last night's window fans to fill the house with rain-washed air and send chills down my bare arms this morning as I stand in the kitchen contemplating the nine and ten foot branches now lying in our backyard. Such a powerful thing, invisible wind. The lip of the porcelain sink is cool beneath my fingers, I wait for the coffee to finish. Voices murmur from the radio. I pause...

"What was the hardest thing about my cancer for you, Daddy?" She'd had bone cancer. Her ten year-old voice strong and sweet now, the tremble in his makes my heart stop.

"Seeing you there, honey. So swollen, so many tubes connected to you...." Those thoughts that your mind skitters away from, an agonizing flame of a fear too terrible to even touch upon. Parenthood is the ultimate state of vulnerability.

You could hear the smile on her lips though, as she remembered one of her favorite things. He would buy tattoo pens at the gift store...and turn her scars into a garden. The long one that ran from her sternum to her pelvic bone became the stem for roses, her favorite flower. The one from her feeding tube, a butterfly. He drew over the monsters. He drew her beautiful.

Standing there, tears sliding down my cheek...so convicted. Every life has joy and pain. Some more so than others. But the secret is in the ink of us. How we approach and confront and forgive and leave behind the monsters. How we make gardens from our scars.

Autumn

Autumn carries more gold in its pockets than all the other seasons.
Jim Bishop

Winter is an etching, spring a watercolor, summer an oil painting and autumn a mosaic of them all.
Stanley Horowitz

Marrow

I made soup today. Roasted chicken. And it took six hours. Seriously. I began sometime after the second cup of coffee, but before the third. Pulled the carcass of bones and tendons from the fridge; burnished skin, gelatinous broth congealed to the breast and thighs. Johny Lang, Tracy Chapman, and Nina Simone took turns in the cd player as I listened to the wind blow outside. Something about the cool caress of Autumn's fingers on my cheek leads me to the kitchen every time.

Nearly unconsciously I begin to peel the meat from the bones. Soon this becomes a personal quest; my fingers sliding along calcium lengths, searching out the divots and undulations that hide the sweetest, darkest meat. Peeling back roasted skin to coax tender slices of salty succulence from their place, separating cartilage from bone, sinew from muscle. The meat drops into the bowl, the bones piling in a mound inside the soup pot. Ribs, back, wings...vertebrae. Skeleton abandoned.

Slice of onion, celery ribs with leafy tops, rosemary cut from the chilly planter on the porch - the single lonely herb left next to the brittle husks of basil and crispy sage. Crushed ivory cloves of garlic, black peppercorns tossed into steaming water...the bones sink beneath an aqueous grave. Soft simmering, tempered heat, rosemary mist. Satisfaction permeates my soul as I leave the room with a last glance toward the window slowly filling with lovely steam.

Three hours later…

Delicious carcass and vegetable pulp. Broth with warmth. Depth. Marrow. Drain, chill, skim the fat, smile softly, secretly at the thought of rosemary infused lusciousness. Chopped pancetta into the pot, crisping. Onion, glistening. Fresh celery, carrots, herbs. The broth from lifeless bones, resurrected into liquid gold.

As I stir, I wonder. This afternoon I received a call from a distant friend, we chatted. Upon her asking about my day, I responded,

"I'm making soup." She laughed.

"Like you open the can, right?" she said. I chuckled softly to myself. As I added crushed sage and fresh rosemary, I wondered if she'd ever had soup - real soup. Soup with love and time and marrow in it. Like life, soup is so substantial, so basic. But when was the last time you had soup made from the bone? There is vitality in it. Pain and blood and pulse and joy and movement...life.

Sometimes I feel like Campbells has taken over the planet. Condensed it. The Hallmark channel: "Open can, add one hour of time and the Jack Frost movie and sha-zam - Christmas Eve!" Do you remember actually threading needles, making cranberry popcorn strings for the tree while swapping "favorite Christmas past" tales? Before Macys took over? I truly don't mean to sound old or like some Martha Stewart commercial, but there is something missing...

Instant marriages? No such thing. Instant parenting? *(take one child, add a wireless device and their own tv...)* Friendships, home-making, dinner, holidays - I am internally battling this war against a condensed life. I refuse to give in.

The last step. After the simmer, the softening of vegetable and meat and corn, a cup of cream. Fresh pepper...the aroma fills the house. I go out to get the mail and the 45 seconds it takes to do so - leave me reveling in the warmth of deliciousness as I reenter. Eyes closed...amazing. Marrow.

Burns

I burned myself last week. I've had a lot on my mind lately and gazing out the kitchen window, I got a bit lost watching the leaves fall like amber snow upon the lawn. There is something slightly bewitching about the sizzle of a roast; searing before it will be nestled into the pot, draped with onions and herbs, and left immersed in broth to simmer. Something snapped me out of my reverie and turning I reached for the metal tongs now left for long minutes in the flame...

Two inches of the flesh on my palm - the kind of burn that you almost hear before you feel. I must of made a sound as my son was quickly in the doorway. I stood quietly with my hand submerged in the dishtub.

"Are you alright, mum?" he asked. I smiled,

"I will be." For that is the secret, isn't it. No matter how deep the pain, how unbearable it seems as it scrapes and tears and breaks our bodies, our dreams....our souls. No matter the wound, there is the balm of time. The bandage of memory, the antiseptic of grace.

Funny how the physical pain fades so much more quickly than that of the heart. I've come to possess such a tolerance for corporeal injury as to constantly wear a smattering of bruises I've no idea how were acquired, scrapes and cuts that I'm amazed to discover when pointed out by the boys. These are merely the companions to a life of labor; refinishing furniture, installing floors, sanding ceilings precariously perched atop a ladder I'm certain holds a personal dislike of me. And then there is the treacherous land of the kitchen - knives and fire do not mix well with hurry and distraction.

I didn't want to look at my hand. To see it somehow makes it hurt more, doesn't it? Kind of like mulling over an insult or argument. I sprayed on the Bactine *(I believe we own four bottles of this magic mist - even keep one in the car...this probably says something about our family)*, covered it with gauze, and returned to finish getting dinner started. *Oh, how it burned!* Seemed about to ignite the bandage, did it rage so. I bit my lip, tears in my eyes, though perhaps it was due to the onions I sliced.

Life goes on. There would be hungry children lingering about in three hours and there was still potatoes to mash and laundry to fold and floors to sweep and... That second hand ticks and the clock turns.

I wish there was a Bactine for the heart. Sometimes a single sentence uttered in anger lingers so long as to tattoo itself on the walls of my mind. I wish I was better at dismissing, banishing these things to the woods where they would be lost amongst the ferns and trees, so much mulch. I'm not.

Then again, if I were, perhaps I wouldn't be as careful at guarding my own tongue. I am conscientious to an extreme, painstakingly so, of the agony unscrupulous words can induce. We all must live with the tragedy we cause...some learn from the past, some do not. I have made mistakes I care never to repeat. This tapestry of life is woven of a million threads. We choose the colors.

It's raining today. The green of summer is fading, relinquishing life to give birth again in spring. As I type I can feel the pull of the new skin on my hand. The damaged tissue cracked and peeled, now replaced by soft pink flesh. Unlined still, its tenderness is a constant reminder for me. Not only to be more prudent where I choose to daydream, but that I am stronger than I sometimes feel. That healing is innate as much as of will...that new flesh, new hopes, and new mornings await.

You Dirty Girl

Spray paint is from heaven, simply put. The defacement of thousands of walls is a small price to pay for the absolutely *magical* ability to take a decrepit piece-o-crap bookcase banged about since college *(grimy white with the bottom four inches stained ew-ish when the basement flooded three years ago)*, and with two cans of "Satin Espresso," create a brand spank-me new darling cabinet that tucked into the 2nd floor bath next to the claw foot tub *(which I also spray-painted)* and VOILA! Bath Divine!

Today was lovely. 80* and sunny, the autumn breeze sending golden leaves dancing through the air as I sprayed away in the backyard. Unbeknownst to me, this playful draft was also sending clouds of Satin Espresso across my yard, surprising me with a "misty" paint job on the rear porch (*whoops*) and tomato plants that now look as if someone sneezed chocolate on them. The dog wised up and bolted for the house.

Five hours later I had proudly arranged my bath, done three loads of laundry, vacuumed, watered plants and chopped veges for dinner. The boys walked in from school and I shooed them quickly out the door – they both had dentist appointments asap. We dashed to the office where I sank gratefully onto the plush couch to relax with the latest edition of *People* for 45 minutes while teeth were polished and sealed.

Our dentist is...rather posh. The eggplant colored walls of the waiting room were accented with a lush mossy green tone that paired wonderfully with the leather furniture, electric fireplace, and bookcases housing nifty statues and old volumes of Shakespear. They don't just clean teeth folks, they look elegant while doing it.

In the midst of this splendor, I suddenly realized the little girl waiting with her mother next to me was whispering and pointing… at *me*. I smiled, certain she just noticed my red hair or glasses. Then her mother suppressed a look of confused horror and grabbing her daughter's hand, moved to the *farthest seat possible* from me. WTH?

I start down the mental list: deodorant this morning, check. No "bra dysfunctions" baring all, check. *(what, this never happens to you?)* No dog poo on the shoes, check. And then I see it. My arm - my ENTIRE right arm has been "cloud painted" a smashing Satin Espresso leaving the impression, if one didn't know otherwise, that not only was I dirty - *I was downright filthy.* I'd had so much to do and yes, I'd washed my hands but I wasn't really paying attention, and I......oh no.

Fighting the blush I knew was raging across my face, I stumbled to the poshy restroom and stared at myself in the tasteful gilt-framed mirror. The entire right half of my face was spotted brown. Down my neck....even a lovely drip-o thing right at my jawline, implying that I was not only dirty, but sticky too. *Was that a moth glued to my hair?*

There is no handsoap on the planet that removes spray paint. But oh, did I try. Now I was blotchy *and* dirty. Pulsating red, plague-like splotches covered my face, and a lovely welt had risen on my neck where I had attempted to scrape off the drip with my fingernail...dear God, I was a walking extra for Contagion.

I slunk out to the waiting room and snatched a magazine to

hold in front of my face. A handsome man named "Brent" was greeted cheerfully by the receptionist before he came to find a seat. The frantic manner in which he backed away from me, nearly landing in someone's lap, said it all. It was a long 45 minutes. I was a dirty girl and there was no denying it.

Metamorphosis

Someone once told me, "a *person* can make good decisions, but people are stupid." I rebelled. My generally optimistic, the damn-glass-is-half-full *(hopefully of whiskey)* nature leans toward assuming the best. I've been known to spout "maybe he's just lost" reasoning as to why the idiot in traffic cut me off nearly impaling my front teeth on the steering wheel as he whipped across three lanes to an exit leaving paint on the guardrail. He just didn't SEE me, right? That awful woman in the market just 'had a bad day.' The bagger at the grocery that smashed your bagels in with your fabric softener so your breakfast tasted vaguely of fabreeze just wasn't "trained right."

But then – an alarming awakening. It started when I decided to pick up some Swanson's frozen deal for my grandmother and discovered the words, "Do not eat the plastic film" on the box. Are you serious? *The film?* I thought that was the best part! Gives a luminescent glaze to the little carrots and a tangy zip to the chicken. I actually considered calling Susie Swanson and telling her that the film was delicious and JUST because I hadn't moved my bowels in two weeks was NO reason to keep me from enjoying it!! Alas, I didn't.

And then last week the boys brought their report cards home. While I am indeed blessed to have honor roll children - I sat in silent stupefication *(is that a word?)* reading the accompanying note:

Tips For A Successful Parent Teacher Conference

1. Arrive promptly or even a few minutes early. Ummm...you're only given a 15 minute slot so being "late" would be bad, right? We all learn that lesson every time we think explicit homicidal thoughts while sitting in the Doctor's waiting room for a 3:30 appointment with a screaming snot-nosed child at 4:15 because some other inconsiderate parent was late. Death to those who can't tell time.

2. Begin with positive comments about the teacher or classroom. Wow. What kind of moldy rock did you crawl out from beneath that you don't know how to say hello nicely? What prompted this lovely social tip - Mr. Thomas walked in and said, "Nasty place this room, and you're as ugly as Billy said you were."

3. Keep your emotions under control. It's a postal society, I know - but in the midst of the insanity, who "loses control" over a second grader's report card?? Exactly HOW many emotional escapades does it take to inspire such an admonition? (*and do I need to move if this is a regular occurrence at our school?*)

4. Be open-minded to suggestions from the teacher. Well....gosh darnit, she is *the teacher*! If she thinks your kid needs to work harder on his handwriting - she's probably right. Rocket science, this is.

5. Express appreciation for the conference. Again, *who raised you??* Show appreciation for the person who puts up with your little demon 40 hours a week while attempting to educate him so he's not living in your basement when he's 35? **DEAR GOD, *say thank you!***

And it occurs to me - damn, people are really....just stupid. Not in the uneducated "good-hearted-but-can't-pour-piss-out-of-a-boot-if-the-directions-were-on-the-heel" kind of way *(you can thank my southern mother for that one)*; but in a self-centered, oblivious, don't-even-SEE-you-on-the-radar kind of way. Where has this general dysfunction come from? When did parents stop teaching their children to say hello, listen while someone is speaking, and thank them for their time? And then these children grew up...and now they've spawned.

We have to be told not to eat the plastic wrap. Technology advances, entertainment soars, comfort is supreme...and we're losing our humanity. Our common sense is evaporating as quickly as our common manners. Just standing in line at the bank is an education in trendy swear words. You'd think that having to wait ten minutes *for your turn* while a slightly flustered employee who is obviously trying to do a good job hurries about - is reason to flip out and lose control. Then again, if it can happen over a report card...

Self-control. Patience. Respect. These strands that weave a group of random people into a community - I feel like I'm watching them fray. Has the cocoon of our independent lives left us not with magnificent wings, but crippled, scuttling about on the ground? We're secluding ourselves as surely as a plump caterpillar wraps itself in silk. We don't need to interact with *anyone* to shop for clothes, order pizza...pay our bills, invest in the market - even go to school or work. But within that cocoon I fear we may be shriveling rather than growing.

    I want butterflies. I want to see my children soar. If it takes all my strength and all my days - I will never settle for rude. Never allow the stupid, the insolent...the loss of the very thing that makes man so capable of wonders. I will battle to have sense and manners become common again.

Anew

Like the way your fingers tingle upon the touch of a new lover's flesh, so my hands feel. Trembling with excitement, slightly terrified and more than a shade awkward. It's been nearly five months...

I was devastated. Even now my heart pounds as I think about that day. My hands curl slightly - that feeling in your stomach like you've fallen a great distance. One hundred and forty-nine days since. One hundred forty-nine days without unscrewing a tube of paint. A summer packed full of children and trips to the pool and long evenings spent reading on the front porch. Every so often I would wander into my studio and just breathe. Liquid sunshine, the smell of charcoal and paint and wooden canvas frames would roll over me like warm ocean waves. I would run my fingers over the soft brushes that waited patiently in the empty teapot. And quietly leave.

Truly it's unlike me to be so cowardly. But there it is. I was afraid. Oh, so robust of me to use the past tense there - because I am *still* afraid. It's difficult to explain the uncertainty that has taken root in my heart. Even with hundreds of canvases behind me, well, they were all painted with *that* brush. The one now a solid concrete mass of unrecoverableness.

School commenced and I found myself preparing for our annual bash, the Soup. This is quite the undertaking as we open the entire house to guests; every bedroom, bathrooms, the mancave in the basement as well as the third floor library and my studio. You know how when you have friends over there's always a room you shove crap in and shut the door? We can't do that when expecting so many which forces me to de-clutter and clean every scrap and nano-meter we live in. A tad overwhelming, but heck - I'm done cleaning till after the holidays!

The Soup was a week ago and a part of me cringed the entire evening as I was faced with the same inquiry over and over,

"So what have you painted lately?" Ummmm.....nothing? Everything from early spring has sold so what was left on the walls was older; ones I don't like enough to hang or cannot part with for some reason or other. Mixing the chocolate chips into the pancake batter the next morning, I came face to face with the apprehensive artist now living in my home. She gazed at me from the reflection in the kitchen window.

Sunday and Monday were party-recovery. *(dear Lord above, I am not twenty anymore)* Tuesday and Wednesday I cleaned and cooked. And this morning I sent the boys off to school, tidied up...and pulled on my gear. Clothes ancient, covered in paint and ink. Dabs of olive green and ocher, cobalt blue and crimson; the rip in the right leg gaps a bit, framing the skin of my knee in a strange motley way.

It took eleven brushes. They just felt wrong in my hands. I kept switching them, one into the teapot after another, the splash of water a harsh reminder of my neglect. Later I sat, this painting staring back. It's not large, only 10 x 12 or so, and this is just the first stage. The part where I force my mind back into my dreams and attempt to pull them out and make them tangible. Sometimes I love my work best at this stage, for here they appear much more like real dreams, blurry, the edges undefined. From here though, my waking mind clarifies, delineates and eventually finishes the work. If I like it, it lives. If I don't, well there is always gesso.

Starting over. Something the human race is renowned for. Our ability to adapt and accept transitions, to forge on after overwhelming loss. Relationships, marriages, parenting. New jobs, new challenges - life after abandonment, disease, and graveyards. I suppose my fear is really founded in my own selfish aversion to change, my comfort in how it was. Some roads we find ourselves upon are not our choice but each leads someplace from where we are. Here's to knowing I don't want to stay where I am....so one foot in front of the other. I begin.

Sexy

Yesterday afternoon my nine year-old came running into the house to tell me there was some wild bug in the back yard I just *had* to see. He grabbed my hand, pulling me toward the door while I was laughing and trying to dry off with a kitchen dishtowel; leaving a half carved chicken on the counter. We were almost to the door when he stopped and turned my hand over to look at the palm. His fingers were gentle as he touched the rougher thickened spots.

"Mom, what are these?" he asked.

"Calluses, honey, you get them from working hard." I said.

"Why do you work so hard Mom?"

"Cause your daddy thinks it's sexy."

Sexy. What a universe is contained within such a small word. It encompasses ideas so varied, so open to interpretation - googling it may be more frightening than educational. In this crazy maze of variety and taste, *(yes, I did once find a calendar in my college roomie's closet - smack me now - it had very large men in very lacey lingerie. I considered lysoling my eyes)* the idea of what is "sexy" is as varied as the proverbial fish in the sea.

There is a woman I pass frequently in the grocery aisles. I probably pass the same 58 people on a regular basis and never realize it - however she is a tad memorable. Possibly a distant relative of Mimi on the Drew Carey Show, she has a passion for ice-blue eye shadow, meticulously applied orange lipstick, and garish Hawaiian print dresses. She resembles Mimi in more than just appearance, I might add. I nearly swallowed my gum when rounding a corner to hear her say to a small boy, "Ya little cracker, takin' up space with yer stupid boots, move it!" While I'm sure she has an endearing sweet side, the ensuing verbal battle between Mimi-twin and Cracker-mom was enough that I skipped the baking isle that day. Cake is simply not worth that particular mess.

But what occurred to me, was that sometime *that very morning*, she stood in front of a mirror before she left the house and thought, "Damn, I look good!" Most likely she has a husband who thinks she is the *cat's meow*...and I am truthfully rather grateful for this! The older I get, the more I realize that if everyone liked the same thing, half the planet would be out of luck. Which brings me back to sexy. I really wasn't kidding when I told my son that yesterday…

It was August. You could taste the heat, like salt and yellowed grass and pavement. I had been in my studio painting. My hair pulled up, I had paint - as usual - everywhere. My hands, my neck, my tank top was smeared with the colors of sky and sand. I smelled like acrylics and sweat. When I answered the door he said, "God, you're sexy." I laughed. And then we promptly forgot about going out to dinner.

I was raised on a ranch which resulted with a hard ass case of physical labor addiction. Two days ago I spent nearly nine hours sanding and painting the entire front *porch (which looks smashing, I must say)* and am still sitting here with bruised knees and slivers in my fingers. But I love it. I adore the ache in my legs and the stiff muscles of my back after a hard day of work. And when nine times out of ten, he comes home to me in drywall dust or dirt or paint…

I know, I know - how can anyone find that sexy? He does. And this sweat inspired arousal is certainly not one directional! I'll never forget the day, we had been married only a few months, and he had to change the fuel pump in his truck. One of those things that you think will take 2 hours and it takes 6. He came in covered with grease and oil and gasoline...I handed him a beer. And then knocked it to the floor as I nearly tackled him. He now jokes about making a cologne called "Hard Labor" that smells of a garage. I get a little breathless just thinking about it.

However, it raises the question: do we find only the aroma of hard work attractive - or is it more than that? Could it be possible that the very IDEA of a man working hard, who accomplishes things, makes/builds/fixes things - productivity and creativity and sacrifice - that this is what flips my switch? In a world of couch potatoes and complainers, this dude throws down some scraped knuckles and damn, I melt! Perhaps my pheromones have met my perspicacity? Intelligence encounters lasciviousness…

Hang on, he's just turned off the lawnmower - catch ya later!

Echoes

Upon my easel is a piece of plywood. It has never hung in a gallery, never been the focus of attention, never even noticed. Yet this board is more important, more tangible than my greatest painting. It has seen my soul.

Against it I place my canvases. Gleaming white, they stare blankly back at me, emptiness embodied. I sit across the room tapping my brush against a paintless pallet...waiting. The tornado in my mind, the lists of things undone, the voices of siblings and friends and children must fade. A sip of wine...

A flash. A dream. The music surges and I reach for the plastic tubes of color that litter the shelf. A soft curl of pigment slides into the divot. My hand hovers....

Joy, pain, love. Searching, hiding. Frustration and anger and ecstasy. The emotions of my life spill onto the ivory space, smearing into the images trapped inside of me. The board has seen it all. My sighs of delight at the perfect capture of morning sun; sailoresque swearing at a ruined forest glade. Sometimes I dance when I paint. Sometimes I throw down my brush and leave in fury.

Echoes of every painting I've done are on that board. I can trace them with my fingers. I recognize the color of that ocean sky last year...the black of the cave, the vineyard's emerald leaves. These memories are there - but only for me. It's just nonsense to the world. Like the coffee mug only you know the meaning behind. The last necklace your mother gave you before she died. That picture taken on vacation moments before the disastrous fight you wish you could take back...only you know.

I wonder at the echoes I'm leaving in my life. In my children, my neighborhood. Do I leave remnants of myself? Fingerprints that stain? On one hand I desperately want to change the world - paint it richer and brighter for my sons....and on the other I would give anything for a giant eraser to rub out my mistakes and impatience. The echoes of me. I wonder what they say.

Gators and Poptarts

Yesterday morning I was confronted with absolute proof that my darling angelic boys have horns. And possibly a tail. I suppose every parent at some point faces the human fallibility of their prodigy, but mine slapped me in the face at 8am; shortly after waffles and kisses and "have a nice days." I waved good-bye as they left for the bus, one by one, and then went to tinkle. *(three cups of coffee before dawn will do that to a woman)* And there, staring at me from the bottom of a yellow pool...was Pebbles. Not Bambam, not Fred or Wilma. Pebbles. Someone had ditched their morning vitamin and forgot to flush. Oooooh, I was peeved.

A peeved mum in our house leads to lost allowances and days without television...and cold cheese sandwiches for dinner. *(seriously, ask my boys, tick me off badly - especially by being ungrateful - and I completely go on strike)* Three growing boys used to home cooked menus containing bacon wrapped roasts, homemade bread, and scalloped potatoes suddenly reduced to cold sandwiches and apples will surprise and delight you with *rapid* apologies and changed behavior.

At any rate, confrontations were had, the culprit confessed and handed over the cost of a bottle of Flinstones *(about two week's allowance)* and promises of future honesty were made. When we don't like something, we discuss. We don't lie, cheat or steal....*or flush hard earned money down the toilet, dammit!*

However, last night I was shocked repeatedly as glaring examples of exactly that - lying, cheating, & stealing - were paraded across the television screen accompanied by a catchy tune, nifty tag lines, and the ever-present laugh track. Welcome to American advertising.

Example 1. Sad boy is about to ingest deplorable poptart when he is rescued by generous girl from such a blunder by her offer to share her delish toaster strudel. How does sad boy respond to this kindness? He snatches both halves of the strudel and runs off yelling, "You can have the poptart!"

Example 2. Famous race car driver is "insured for almost everything" by some insurance company but when he accidentally drives a golf ball through someone's window; famous-wealthy-adult race car driver sneaks off.

Co-workers steal each other's food, wives belittle their husbands, and little Timmy in "time out" plays like madman in the kitchen with no supervision. Twenty minutes of any "tween" show on Nick or Disney elevates destructive behavior, deceit, and theft *(all draped in the absolute stupidity of any adult in the room)* to entertainment. And the laugh track runs.

There will always be the discussion about media reflecting reality or dictating it, but I cannot help but wonder as we are setting our children down for "entertainment" that is full of mean girls, moronic adults, and a complete lack of responsibility - how can we expect anything different in our own living rooms?

Well, I refuse to give in. Again. I will block channels our neighbors watch, rampage like a lunatic about stolen yogurt commercials, and attempt to find creative ways to make the consequences fit the crime. Sometimes I feel like I'm piloting a cruise ship on a tranquil sunny sea; other times I'm barely poling my raft of ruffians in a hurricane while alligators snap at my heels.

Parenthood. Why they make whiskey.

Appreciation

I was standing in line at the grocery store. It was the middle of the afternoon on a sunny September day; one of those crisp days, like apple pie and autumn rain. I had filled my grocery cart with roots to roast - turnips and parsnips and sweet potatoes. Fresh rosemary, a loaf of garlic bread, brie to wrap in pastry and bake, and I arrived at check-out. Three lines open, two carts in each - throw the dice, right? I park. Now, I might add to this mental picture that the attached liquor store was having a "tasting" which meant I had three choices of merlot to sample as I waited...yum. However, it was very shortly apparent that things were amiss.

The cashier was in his early 20's. Kinda scruffy, rugged around the edges; well mannered, but in need of a good meal. He was polite, nice, and visibly tired. And the two carts in front of me...wow. Soon after my first sip of a dark Californian blend I noticed - she was swearing at him. She was the same age as he. There was a baby in the cart. She had a pack of WIC *(women, infants & children – vouchers for specific food like milk and cheese)* checks in one hand and a cell phone in the other. She ridiculed him. It was so obvious he was new, nervous. She was that "pretty" that had faded, paled beneath the cruel heat of life. Highlights a little too white, black eyeliner a little too thick, cherry lips that pulled back over viciously sharp teeth, ready to bite. She asked if he was stupid. She joked about his blush with the girl behind her who also had a stack of checks and an 'access' card.

His pain was palpable. It radiated from his reddened cheeks

as he struggled to put the numbers in the system, calculate the credit, scan the specific food. He cringed as he told her the juice she had chosen wasn't covered, and physically cowered as she raged at him. When it was all done and he had fed her checks into the register, she asked for four packs of cigarettes and pulled out a wad of 20's to pay for them.

I gripped the bar of my cart so hard I knew I would have bruises later. She sneered. She laughed with the girl behind her - this one also in her twenties, with two kids hanging on the sides of her cart and her belly stretched tight with a third, she swore. Language that made me gasp - actually out loud - so that they both looked at me. She tossed her cheese and milk carelessly on the belt,

"What, you got a problem with that??" As the previous director and executive director of numerous early childhood centers and preschools - I was speechless. Dumbfounded. Outraged. I fumbled. Me, with what I've done, the places I've been, I *fumbled*. I stepped back. At this point it had been 25 minutes. I'd watched four other people get in line behind me...observe...check out the other lines...then smile almost apologetically, and move over. I watched them leave. There was some part of my mind that was screaming for me to just SWITCH LINES! What on earth was the big deal?? Just "move along."

But there was a day. One day. During a warm, indian summer year - when a single mom with worn out sneakers, a cranky toddler and a hungry three year-old stumbled into the welfare office waiting room 4 minutes before her appointment. She wiped the tears from her cheeks. She was horrified. Three months ago she was a stay-at-home mom. A wife. Safe.

That caseworker told me I was what she lived for. That I was someone who had worked since I was 17 and had paid into this system and that is was a pleasure to help me when I really needed it. She was amazing. She took one of the most humbling, awful moments in my life and filled it with kindness. I have never been so grateful. So thankful. With that green plastic card came the ability to feed my boys meat. Doctor appointments and immunizations. I could stop selling plasma.

I have stood in many lines WIC checks in hand, cheese and milk and juice - and never fathomed ridiculing the person who's very taxes were paying for my meals. I stood humbled, appreciating every mouthful of food, every gulp of milk.

Four months and my life was different. I signed a lease, a contract. I sold a painting, began teaching again. I smiled as I hugged my caseworker and told her goodbye. I was done. Years have gone by now. For every frightened mother that I have held, connected to services, and cheered on as they landed on their feet, for every proud and hungry parent I have urged in the direction of help even when it hurt. For every moment that I have understood people who are struggling - I have been grateful for that time. There is no replacement for walking in a pair of shoes.

But what have we become? How is it that there is a wave of people that ridicule those of us that work forty, fifty hours a week - god awful black, cold, early mornings…late nights comforting your son because you missed his Christmas play to handle an employee emergency? How did that happen? I have LIVED the life of a "family supported." I have *been* there. Not for a moment, a single *instant* did I not know that the food on my child's plate came from the table, the paycheck, the taxes of someone who got up and *went to work*.

I raise my boys now. I watch them....watching me. How do I teach them this? *How do we teach appreciation?* I've been told that appreciation is the child of "without." Doing without - is this the seed? For every day you go without the jeans that everyone else had in 7th grade, is this what makes them magical? Every day you eat hamburger helper - isn't that what makes lobster heavenly? Every lonely night makes the arms of a loved one priceless.

Every day you sell plasma and give your kids mac and cheese for breakfast. Is there a waiting period? How do you take a significant portion of our society and make them understand what it is to do without…when they never do.

I'm truly lost here. I stood in that line. For an hour. When I started unloading the lukewarm milk and brie from my cart, the cashier said to me, "If you're WIC, get out of my line." I smiled. I told him he was doing an excellent job. His shoulders unknotted. He turned, watching their carts as they left. I wanted to tell him they weren't normal. That they weren't what we were working for. He and I, standing together on a warm fall afternoon...wondering what the world was coming to.

Whys and Hows and Cake

A phone call. Someone close to me, separated from her spouse, fighting her way through a new world of two jobs and daycare and lonely single parenthood. Long talks in the past of ifs and maybes and might-have-beens...but now there is only now. And she mentions that she recently asked him, "Why?" Perhaps the most important question - while somehow being simultaneously the most insignificant as it applies to life *now* because no matter WHY, we are indeed now...here. We clutch at the why to justify and explain and soothe the now that is here - when really the why is often a ferris wheel of rationalizations that leave us blinking in the glare of fairy lights, unsure where the beginning or the end might be.

The why can be lethal. It can eat at you, endlessly gnawing at the edges of the reasons you once told yourself. The reasons that made sense. In this cake we are all baking - the life we are writing as we open our mouths and pen the words that sketch the picture within that we live...the ingredients matter.

Time. Dear God, the author of such, time is the blood of life. Giving time, taking time, putting aside time. The vampire that is the twenty-first century is poised, clutching the edge of your tattered calendar, fangs sharp and at the ready. Beware lest he wrench that which you love away.

Thought. Oh yes, acknowledge the power of the mind, for it stands between you and the emptiness that awaits just over there - just past uncaring and self-centeredness. Somewhere beyond "I didn't know" and before "I don't care" lies a terrible black swamp of

"I forgot." O ye who have no ears...

Ah, time and thought are excellent beginnings, the magnificent starters of the race. Look, their legs so long, their muscles strong and sleek, but do you know who wins the final lap?

Effort. The sweaty companion that doesn't sit down, doesn't rest. Effort is the one who takes the thought and makes the time. He pushes past "I'm tired" and "what now" and thrusts himself to the finish line of "it matters."

"He didn't really want to be married...it was too much work." I shudder at the world I see being built around us. Where the tower of a lasting relationship is replaced by the motel 6 of convenience. Where it seems many would rather pitch a tent than get dirty, scrape some knuckles, and lay the stones of a foundation.

It's not just her or him - this story has been written in the marrow of husbands and wives and children. It is not a matter of gender or age, but within the skin of us. I ask you today to just pause amidst the pulse of your life, the rhythm you've become accustomed to. Assess your time, your thought, and your effort.

You, alone...measuring the ingredients. No one wants the cake to fall.

Soup Afterglow

Within the plastic isolated globes where we have all begun to live, our wireless connections weaving tangled patterns in an invisible sky, sometimes I feel I'm holding my breath. Waiting for human contact. Warmth. Flesh. And so as the evenings begin to freeze and we dig out the sweaters and flannel, every year I rebel. Rise up all ye dismal and grey! Denounce thy autonomous ways and come hither....to SOUP!

Yes, this year was the eigth annual North Hills Soup - a party inspired by the hearty, the liquid, the creamy, marrow-infused, herb sprinkled, luscious joy that is soup.

For weeks I search for new recipes, tweak old ones, simmer and bubble my afternoons away in our tiny kitchen. *(not kidding there - one of this year's quotes was "This is a one-butt kitchen!")* I force my family to eat the rejects, harass the neighbors to taste new ones, and whittle the list down to four or five winners. This year I made a spicy Thai peanut shrimp with lime and cilantro, sausage beer & cheese with Guinness and chorizo, a butternut bisque, a hot red chili, and a smoky cream of potato with all the cheese, crumbled bacon, and chives you could load on. *(lovely pals brought a traditional wedding soup and a delish matzah ball creation to round out the menu)*

The invites are a simple postcard I design each year that read: "Bring a bowl, a spoon and a friend. Kids, wine, bread and cheese welcome!" *(it's like a contest with the bowls - one year a rather clever fellow brought a muffin tin so he could eat six soups at a time,* last year the dog food bowl was a hit, and this year it was a tie between the transformer cereal bowl and the finding Nemo complete with a hinged lid and flippy tail) We start at seven and end when the last guest is satiated - usually around 4am. It's a simple "Come when you can, leave when you must" that can be worked around other engagements and leaves everyone happy while spreading the guest load throughout the evening.

 The music is smashing as my husband is a genius at mixing Santana with the Muppets and Moby. From Prince to Michael Buble', Chemical Brothers to Martin Sexton & CC Adcock - it's an eclectic surge of auditory pleasure. There's a guest book to sign and a basement with video games and foosball for the kiddos. Piles of bread and baked brie and goat cheese and scrumptious vittles cover the dining room table as everyone brings something to add; the buffet holds dozens of bottles of wine, and the line into the kitchen for your next bowl is an excellent place to meet new friends and catch up with old ones.

 We always awake the morning after to a house full of kids that are not our own. I finish off the merlot while making a mountain of pancakes and bacon, dancing to the still-playing music. Last year we had over 120 Soupers and I've yet to read through the guestbook, but last night was a fantastic collection of intellect, wit, and charismatic souls that laughed and danced and connected in a tradition of simplicity and pure, warm, human contact.

 I relish the Soup. It revives me, reminds me that the world is made of flesh and breath, not manufactured compounds and synthetic fibers. Our house is not grand, the unfinished trim of a doorway incomplete, the paint chipped in the hall - but this does not hinder our festive camaraderie. For the truth of the Soup, the revelation, is that if you wait until "it" is done - whatever your "it" may be - you will miss out on the authentic happiness that is "now." We all have scuffs and brokens and imperfects...but this is *exactly* what ties us together! Soup takes the scraps and leftovers and odds and bits and makes sustenance and joy – and if you're lucky, there's croutons. And cheese, always cheese.

Ps. I know of at least seven other "Soup" parties now hosting an annual gathering – three countries, all across the states. What are you waiting for?

This seems an excellent opportunity to pass on two of my most cherished recipes…

Bacon Brittle

1 C sugar

1/2 C light corn syrup

1/3 C water

1 C whole cashews

1 lb bacon

1-2 Tbsp butter

2 tsp vanilla

1 tsp baking soda

Preheat oven to 375*, spread nuts on sheet and bake for 6-8 minutes, till just browned. *(don't skip this - makes them WAY more flavorful!)* Cool. Attempt not to eat them all.....in fact, better roast at least 1/2 cup more than needed as, once toasted, they are hard to resist.

Fry bacon till crispy, drain and cool, chop/crumble. Chase spouse from room with hot spatula - you WILL need all of it!

Once cooled, chop nuts roughly and add to bacon - set aside.

In saucepan, combine sugar, corn syrup and water. Heat over LOW heat until sugar has dissolved - may stir a bit.

Once sugar has dissolved, turn heat to high and DO NOT STIR. Mixture will begin to turn an amber color. *(the depth of color is up to you. "light brown sugar" or darker for deeper flavor. Experiment, a good rule for life)*

While mixture is cooking - spray a cookie sheet lightly with cooking spray. *(not a bad idea to spray an extra wooden spatula or spoons to use as spreaders)*

Once mixture has turned amber, remove immediately from heat and add baking soda, vanilla, butter, cashews & bacon. *(it will foam a bit from the vanilla - mix quickly and be careful!)*

Dump onto greased cookie sheet and use coated spatulas to QUICKLY spread out. Allow to cool, then snap into pieces. *(I blot any excess oil off the back of the candy with a paper towel after it cools, before breaking)*

Make two batches....hide one. Use as currency.

Home Made Syrup

Melt: 1 Cup of butter

Add: 2 Cups of brown sugar

    6 Tbsp milk or cream

    Small pinch of salt

When mixture begins to boil, remove from heat and add:

    1 pint white karo syrup

    2 tsp vanilla

Pour into a jar/pitcher that can fit in your microwave – it will solidify in the fridge, just heat and stir to serve. Excellent on ice-cream, waffles, and a perfect hostess gift!

Heartbeat

The air smells like spring seduced late summer and drenched the night in promises. Somewhere between possibility and substance, the evening hovers, a strange shade of autumn. The clouds seem darker.

I nudged his knees apart as he sprawled on the creased coffee brown leather couch, remote in hand. The speckling of pin pricks over his shoulder a silent reminder of the Christmas kitten that filled my heart with joy and, years later, with grief as I buried him.

"What's up?" he murmured as I sank down, my hip fitting into the space above his. My shoulders dropped slowly towards his chest. I swear the night paused as my abdomen curled, my head dipped, and his heartbeat became the universe.

The thud that embodies tomorrow, no matter the anxiety of today. The literal fading of 'to do' lists and apprehensions and doubt. Thump, thump, thump. Breathe.

Footsteps on the stairs, my fourteen year-old son coming down for a snack before bed. I lay there, the muscular drum echoing in my ear; my hair, uncut since January, tangled about us. Footsteps retreating. Recognition of a moment that, while he may not understand, my eldest knew I needed.

Amazing...astounding what fifteen minutes surrounded by the throb of another's heart can do for the equilibrium of a soul. Storms arrive and abate. The planet spins. And hearts beat.

Blurred

End-of-summer rain traces the outline of the window panes next to me; damp trails glimmering beneath the slate clouds that seem to hover close enough to touch, should I stretch out my hand. September appears in a rush this year, invading August's heat with a wave of chilly nights and cool breezes that have me reaching for a shawl when I retreat to the porch to read. Such a change is quite welcome after the igneous days of July, though I do hope Winter doesn't jump the gun as well. His frozen claws can surely wait for the new year to begin, I pray.

It's rather staggering that the school day routine will be returning in mere days to our home. My, how the summer has flown - so cliche, yet so true. If I force myself to concentrate I can snap a frame into focus - *the taste of fire-boiled coffee clutched in the blue enamel mug, my feet tucked beneath me as I watch the morning mist and breathe in the scent of bacon and smoke...*marvelous, the escape of tents and fireflies and non-electric entertainment. But then, I turn my head and the months are murky again, indistinct. I feel....hazy. Vague.

I've been arguing with a canvas. For days now. It began as any other, shifting dreams that float through my midnight mind, lingering in the morning until I fill the broken teapot with water and smear pigment onto my palette. Damp brushes dried on the old sundress I wear to paint in the summer, the open window whispering rumors of season's end in my ear. A large work, this one - three feet long and two high. Burnt umber and ocher and saffron, topaz and crimson and and gold....autumn dreams spill into my tangible world.

Painting, for me, is a known animal. The beginning: shapes and colors and place. As if you viewed such a scene through an unfocused camera, bleary and undefined. Then it's as if I slowly turn the lens in my mind, a line here, leaves there, and gradually the world shifts into view. But not this one.

I cannot seem to....find it. Hours spent and it stares back at me, shadows and light and color. I can hear the wind when I look at it, smell the damp leaves that have piled around the rocks...but I cannot *see* it.

Granted, these last weeks have been....unnormal. (*is that a word?*) Unordinary? Atypical. Plans made have shifted with a phone call that involved the sentence, "...taken to the emergency room..." The seizure of one's heart these small words can cause, the tilting of the planet. The details of everything muffled with emotion.

Perhaps I just need time. Set it aside and wait a bit. I think I will take it down to the dining room in a few weeks, welcome Autumn as she arrives. Sip wine and share a meal with it....let it rest as we live and love and weep and laugh. Do you think life might seep into it? Permeate the fibers with the vision I do not seem to have?

Appetite

I stood at the stove, wooden spoon in hand, reveling in the beefy goodness saturating the air and condensing into damp whirls upon the kitchen windowpane. Nina Simone crooned from the stereo while the rosemary and sea salt bread crisping in the oven tinged the house with that hominess that I swear only comes from baking something with yeast inside of it. The chaos of the day was slipping slowly into the shadows, dinner was moments away.

"Mom, I'm *starving* - can I have a snack?" My fingers clench for a split second on the wooden handle and my spine stiffens. The woman who has spent two hours on her feet to produce this masterpiece of a meal is slightly offended, but a glance at the six foot two, twelve year-old lanky boy in the doorway restores my sense of humor - seriously, the boy has *always* been hungry.

"Do you know what the most important ingredient is?" I ask, my head tilted slightly, eyes shining, a smile on my lips. He sighs, he's heard this many times. Grinning back, he turns to leave with that resigned slouch of the shoulders, capitulating as gracefully as his growling stomach will allow. "Ten more minutes!" I call after him, chuckling softly to myself. My friends, do you know what the most essential ingredient is? Appetite.

My mother used to tell me this as I too, hung about the kitchen, drooling over the scents escaping the blistering oven. The pots that simmered upon the stovetop, the pies cooling on the sideboard. Ahhh, the delicious joy of aching anticipation. Feeling positively *hollow,* it seemed as if Dad saying the blessing was going to last till dawn, but then that first bite - oh, sweet heaven! Eyes closed, mouth full, utter bliss.

With this holiday season creeping closer, candy stuffed fists knocking on our doors, programs dripping gravy and cheese seeping from our television screens, hypnotic magazine pictures of the ultimate festival of cakedom strewn about our coffee tables - may we take a moment to pause. To evaluate. How hungry are you? I fear the truth of that question may surprise you. For if one is excruciatingly honest, for many of us, *it has been years.*

It's the latest diet fad, hanging about for a while now - the idea that the standard "three meals a day" motif of life was actually straight from the Satanic bible. It's solely responsible for that cushy tush and those darling love handles we all seem to sport....GET THEE AWAY FROM ME, YE SPAWN OF HADES!! Rather you must eat six small meals spread throughout your day, peppered with "healthy snacks" and tiny treats all in the name of: **"Never let yourself get hungry because you lack the self-control to not gorge until reaching the point of belt-loosening expansion."**

But I ask, have we lost more than the odd pound in this quest? We are becoming, in oh-so-many ways, such a society of the moment - waiting for *anything at all*, a thing of the past. On-line shopping, instant downloads, fast food, drive through restaurants *(NOT to be confused with fast food, mind you)* automatic, importunate, split-second life. We multi-task our existence and waiting is a terribly un-vogue ritual spoken of only by those that actually know how to dial a rotary phone.

Desire and yearning. Thirst. Longing, needing, craving. The

friction of a fingertip along the soft skin on inside of your elbow, the absolute most perfect Christmas gift ever found, a love letter written by hand and sprayed with scent that lingers in the mailbox for days, making you smile. Butter melting into the dips and divots of a piece of hot bread, the oven still spilling its yeasty warmth into the kitchen behind you. Each of these, made so much more splendid by the wait. *By the appetite!*

So this year, as your life amps up into overdrive and your schedules begin to collide like planets knocked out of orbit, I challenge you. Don't snack on your way home. Don't indulge every whim, for the very definition of a whim is just a passing fancy. Wait for desire. Be hungry. Life will taste better.

Winter

Winter is not a season, it's an occupation.
Sinclair Lewis

In the depth of winter I finally learned that there was in me an invincible summer.
Albert Camus

The Heart

I usually listen to NPR in the morning while I get ready for the day. Unlike the local news, I relish the global review of the latest whatnot, politics, and events. There is something amazingly humbling in hearing about the devastation caused by the floods in Pakistan and I'm complaining about laundry? The trembling voice of the Chilean miner's wife who is camping in the barren desert in the smallest of tents even now, until her husband can be pulled from the collapsed tunnel he is trapped in - a process that may take *months* - reminds me that while my husband is putting in long hours at the office, *he is coming home tonight.* Sometimes, perspective is everything.

Every Friday there is a segment called Story Corps that airs. A minute or two of dialog between usually two people, often "interviewing" although sometimes it's just one telling their story. This morning it was a married couple. He has Alzheimer's, she is his caregiver. She asked him what he had learned from the disease. He said,

"I have learned that I am not made up of memories or knowledge. I've learned that who I am...*is in my heart.*"

This has hunted me all day. Even as I type now I'm fighting back tears. Who am I...*in my heart*? Am I kind? Critical? Generous...demanding? Who are you in your heart? If you lost all of your knowledge, your memories, your past...if you were *just your heart*...who would you be? With your children, your spouse, your neighbors.

Would I be able to find joy in waking up? In toast and a poached egg and a cup of tea? Could I live inside of one single day without tomorrow, without yesterday? Can you imagine - holding on to no anger, nursing no worries, no fears... just **today**. To be content, in only today.

He sounded happy. Quite stunning really. I think I envied it, even while I ached inside for what he had lost. Perhaps it had been balanced by what had been gained? What is the value of peace? How much does serenity cost?

At the end, his wife said that she had read somewhere that if you loved someone, truly loved them, you would wish to outlive them. You would voluntarily bear the burden of loss and grief and hold them to the end. She wept. She told him she was so glad, so very glad she was there to hold him.

Who she was in her heart...was breathtaking.

Gorilla Girl

You know, today was lovely. Awesomely lovely. Normal in every way as I headed toward Target for miscellaneous crap and cat food. And then...

Two hours later I had retrieved not one, but THREE bottles of shampoo from the top shelf. I nearly dropped some patio planter on my head to the utter joy of the slew of toddlers watching, fetched a box of cereal from a display model, and I put my lower back out shoving Begging Berta's box-o-dishes into her cart.

Do I work at Target? No. Am I a nun out to earn my place in the heavens with good deeds and charity? No. *(did I forget to mention the fifteen minutes I stood with my arms over my head, holding up CURTAINS for this yoda-esque old lady who just "didn't know if they were long enough for my windows deary...")* My day in Target was brought to you by my jeans. No, not "genes." The ones on my derriere with the 36 inch inseam. The saga begins....

My first memory of how absurd the world was going to be was walking into a new classroom in 4th grade and having a complete stranger - an adult - shake my hand. She thought I was the substitute. Seriously. Now remember, this is nearly 30 years ago when they did NOT have "cool kid clothes" in larger styles. Oh, the pictures in my mind, it was frightening. There was lots of polyester. And elastic.

I grew so fast I out-paced every ounce of coordination the good Lord gave me. There wasn't a stairwell I couldn't fall up. Cracks in the sidewalk were like engraved invitations for me to face plant. I misjudged doorways, ate soccer ball nets, and on one brilliant occasion - nearly decapitated myself in my own locker.

And then there was my name. Now seriously, I took French - and I know that it's a French name and that it means "to sing" and all the lovely stuff - but I swear, it's Chan<u>TEL</u>, not Chan<u>TALL</u>. "Hightower" was bad enough - we won't even GO into "Show-n-tell." *(trust me, you get asked out by all the wrong guys...)*

I'd like a dime for every time someone has said to me, "Oh, I'd LOVE to be tall..." Really? You haven't lived until you have wet down a pair of jeans, closed the ankles in the dorm door, and leaned your entire being into stretching them....just....thiiiiiiis....much. Of course, when the roommate opens the doors causing the jeans to whip at light speed through the air leaving rivet marks on your face, the night has just begun.

My chest is eye-level for half of America. My cheeks seem to be magnets, attracting the knife-like little pointy ends of umbrellas city wide. Rainy days are lethal to me if I have to go downtown, I look like I'm dodging a hive of wild bees or trying out for some kind of circus limbo act.

One of my arms is longer than the other; not that this actually matters since there isn't a *single* "off the rack" kinda place I can shop for something long-sleeved. I order everything from a catalog called "Long Elegant Legs." The mail man thinks I'm buying sleezy lingerie....or porn. I understand that the world isn't fair. We each have our own list of things we'd like to change about ourselves. However, I wear a size 12 shoe. Swear. I think I missed my calling. I should have been a bouncer...or worked for Target.

Angels

It was 6:05 on a grey, rainy Tuesday morning. I had recently divorced my first husband and thus was alone in a new apartment, hours from any family and rather isolated from friends. My youngest had his tonsils and adenoids removed a week earlier at the tender sweet age of three, he'd done so well. Opening that bedroom door to crimson blankets and his terrified face nearly stilled my heart. "Mama," he said, blood pouring from his mouth. I think I stopped breathing.

I'd just begun to see the man that would become my husband years later; but at that time we hadn't even officially been on a date. My fingers shook as I dialed his number, there was no one else to call. He canceled his day and was there in minutes, reassuring my other son that everything would be fine; he held Sawyer's hand as they watched Brennan and I leave for the hospital. For the next three days I lay in single railed bed, my body curled around my little boy's as he struggled to accept new blood and remake his own. And for three days a near stranger took care of everything else.

There have been moments in my life when such compassion has left me speechless. "Thank you" is the most inadequate phrase on the planet when your heart is awash with relief and gratitude. In every sense of the word, an angel touched my life.

Fast forward nearly a decade and having just moved into a new neighborhood. Last summer had me banging on my neighbor's door in my bathrobe at dawn, sobbing. I begged them to come watch the boys as the ambulance was on its way and I trembled with fear at the thought of losing the love of my life. Twelve hours later I returned and again, "thank you" wasn't nearly enough. I don't know what I would have done if it weren't for their kindness and that of my dear Ag, who came and took the boys to her home so I could return to my husband's side.

    Yesterday I was the one that was honored to sit in the curtained cubicle as they took the vital signs of a woman I'd only met twice. Her husband has just finished his time with the marines and they moved here a few months ago to begin a new life when my husband hired him. New job, new city. He arrived at the ER, having rushed from work and collected their eldest from school; we were told his wife would be taken by ambulance to another hospital.

    As I set my purse on the table next to their front door, I assured him I'd find the peanut butter to make lunch. He quickly showed me the baby's room and set up the game system for the 7 yr-old. He thanked me with the same look I know had been on my face more than once, and ran to meet the ambulance holding his wife inside.

    I didn't get my errands done, or the shopping, and I have *never been so grateful for that.* I made sandwiches and sliced bananas and played pattycake that left 'nana moosh on my fingers. After I laid the little guy down for a nap, I learned all about Lightening McQueen's race track and new paint job in the x-box game...even got handed the controller when I brought up a bowl of goldfish crackers for snack and was told to "go faster!"

    In this world of unexpected agony, when a phone call can shift the axis of your earth, we need each other to be the hand of

God. We have been trusted with this beautiful planet full of hearts and lives, each woven together to make the glorious tapestry that is humanity - and yet it seems daily we hear the stories of how we tear at one another. Murder and plunder and abuse. Perhaps almost the greater evil, indifference. It's not me. It just happens. When it is you, you will need your angel. Please seek to be what you will one day need.

    Together, we can change the world.

Spa Day

Had a crappy week. Feel crappy, think crappy, dream crappy. Crappy weather, crappy laundry, crappy service at the grocery store *(damn the crappy crooked cart),* crappy bills, crappy phone calls, crappy cat crap. (*wow, didn't even plan that one*) And yes, to top off this mountain of colonic wonder is the fact that I *look* like crap. No amount of reassuring, primping, hair spraying, viewing myself sideways or sucking in my cheeks is going to change that. The complexion went to hell, my "split ends" have split ends leaving my hair a crispy tuft of frizz, and my nails? I could try out for an extra in a "Thriller" video.

So Alice calls and suggests a Spa Day. "A what?" A "SPAAAAA day." A lovely day of scrumptious pampering with lotions, creams, steaming....hmmm...wait, like I have that kind of cash?? Three boys under ten, two birthdays coming up, boy scout fees, school fundraisers, and a youngest child that seems able to wear out a pair of shoes in world-record-breaking time. (*did you eat them?*) There is no money tree in the yard to pay someone to steam my head! But Alice *(dear Alice)* says,

"No honey, you just stay home, don't answer the phone, and do all the little things you wish you had time to do - manicure, pedicure, facial mask, steam your pores, condition your hair - pamper *yourself* instead of everyone else!" Cool. I can do that. Commence Spa Day:

Kiss the kids and hubby goodbye, make an omelet. Egg beaters, green onions, leftover chili and cheese - yum. Coffee with gingerbread creamer - yumm-o. Upstairs to begin! Hmmm…ok, steam the face and OW! Little hot there - mental note: check hot water heater temp. Refocus. Apply clay facial mask guaranteed to "clear all pores and make you glow." Let's see...directions say "let dry." So in the meantime, remove all ancient nail polish and file nails. Apply "cuticle remover." Phone rings. Ignore. Wait - my sister, going through stuff: answer, "hello? yeah...blah blah…" Ow - what the *hell*?

"What is in cuticle remover? ACID?!?!" Ahhhh! Drop phone, mad dash for sink. Trip and smash elbow on door frame. Rinse hands frantically in warm water swearing to send nasty letter to Sally Hansen. Pick up phone. Sister hung up. Try to stick tongue out at phone, realize cannot move mouth. Clay mask has hardened like black top. Back to sink. Rinse. Rinse more...clay in nose hairs. Ow.

Ok, deep breath. Apply "regenerating eye cream." Oooh, soothing! Paint nails with clear base coat while eye cream is absorbing. Crack knee into sink while trying to turn on water to rinse burning eye cream out of eyes without messing up nails. Fail. Swear. Dry face and notice that there are distinct red "moons" surrounding my eyes now. Skip eye cream. Decide to wait on the nails in order to dampen hair and apply the "root stimulating hair conditioning balm." Slippery shit. Fall half in the tub soaking my t-shirt, and the rug. Shut the cat in the door trying to get a towel. Chase cat naked down the stairs in front of the glass front double doors praying to GOD that the mailman is NOT out there in order to check the sucker for broken bones. Cat is fine. Swear loudly. Limp back upstairs.

Repaint base coat on nails. Blow. Succeed in beautiful base

coat!! Yeah! Climb in shower to rinse hair and shave. Fall on ass due to residual coating of hair "balm" in tub. Swear more. Turn on shower, rinse stupid hair for 20 minutes till it doesn't feel like pond slime. Apply "lavender scented" shaving gel and discover the razor is dull. Hang precariously out of shower, soaking the other rug, digging through crap on shelf for extra razor heads - knock new can of hair mousse to the floor where it explodes covering a four foot section of the wall in foam - and the cat. Which goes howling down the stairs streaming foam like a deranged fire extinguisher. Don't bother following. Shave. Love that lavender! Get out and find fuzzy bathrobe to relax in.

Eyebrows. Outta control and distinctly resembling Conan the Barbarian. Tweezers...ow. Careful, careful...just when I'm about to pull - WTH!?! A tail, a damp sticky tail from the cat-a-la-hair-care, whips up under my bathrobe as he's attempting to grab my robe belt....ahhhhh! Crap. *Where is the end of my eyebrow??* Gone. Pulled 17 hairs instead of 3. Uh, whoops? Squint, hmmm...no one will notice, right?

Paint the toes - lovely! Fingernails are a smashing "moonlit evening" and I sit back and CRACK! The lid of the toilet snaps off and I whack my head into the window frame as I collapse into the space between the fabulous porcelain throne and the wall. Swear a *great* deal. Attempt to heave myself up with my elbows to save the nails. Hair snags on wet polish leaving globs of "moonlight" in freshly "root stimulated" hair. Give up. Sit on floor, wet cat staring at me, and cry. Spa day my chemical burned, bruised, banged-up, goose-egged, eyebrow-missing ass.

The kids are home.

"Mom?"

"Go away." The husband comes home, hesitantly knocks on the bathroom door.

"Honey?" Sniff. Door slowly swings open. He stares.

"What, don't I look beautiful after my day at the spa??" I ask, raising half an eyebrow. He hesitates.

"Um......."

Um. That's the total result of my SPAAAAA day. Um. So much summed up in two spectacular letters. I'm going to need a week to recover. The cat is going to need Prozac.

I'm *never* talking to Alice again.

Possessed

Sometimes I have thoughts I would never admit to anyone. Not necessarily because I'm afraid or they're horrible thoughts, just that they are so out of character for me, so far from who the world knows me to be. This week I was headed for work. (*I've picked up something a few days a week as my studio is as frigid as a witch's t...ah yes, you can fill in the blank there. Needless to say, no painting is possible.*) And on that journey downtown, I pass several piles of blankets-o-homeless. The carefully assembled, mindfully arranged mountain of cloth indicating a slumbering soul beneath the overpass. This week...I envied them.

From a distance, perhaps even from right next door, everything is fine. And in truth - it is. Honestly, I have an amazing husband and three marvelous boys and a dog that can drive me mad but still waits on the bathroom rug while I shower, she loves me so. We purchased our home two years ago from the same place we bought our washing machine. Imagine that - Craig's list is quite handy, and this huge hulk of a century old house had the bones that I've dreamt about. Eleven foot ceilings, three fireplaces, stained glass and a front porch we dance and eat, play chess and linger on long into the summer evenings. Of course, the *months* of me wearing drywall dust as an accessory, sporting the fragrance of primer and wood stain, sawdust in my hair and paint on my cheek as I made dinner have taken a toll. But we've made a home quite lovely through sweat and tears and occasional swearing.

However, every once in a while, amidst the scheduling and

juggling and arranging and cleaning and disciplining and chasing and stocking...and cleaning again. I just get tired a bit...inside. I think we all do. Life can be heavy. I'm quite religious about clearing out the clutter, passing on what we don't need; (*especially if irked, my husband comes home to a missing coffee table and empty shelves and immediately inquires, "Is something amiss?"*) but at times I wonder if I have possessions...or if I am possessed.

The human dilemma: how much is enough? The years I spent in Guatemala and Mexico, I lived out of two boxes. One of clothing - all dresses, of course; *(thus began my love affair with the sundresses I now live in during the sultry months of summer)* and the other filled with books. I also carried a camera in my bag and a set of water colors. That was it. I am slightly stunned by that.

I'm writing this with my laptop resting in the antique secretarial desk I received for mother's day some years ago. Atop of it is a potted rosemary plant I brought in for the winter, several of the aged hardbound books I adore, a bronzed lamp with an amethyst trumpet flower shade, various stationary and journals - there are more objects within my reach as I sit here, than I owned then. Of course children come with their own apparatus; the tackle box it takes to raise three boys is crammed with pocket knives, band aids, and legos. Add a husband and a pup and my world is overflowing. Creating a sanctuary they can all run to is a mother's job, I know this. So am I insane that once in a while, for a split second of a moment, I wish to just keep driving? Dear Lord, not forever - but for a day? A week?

Perhaps I need a vacation. Or more sleep. I do take comfort

in the fact that most of what we own we have rescued from curbs and garages, spending weeks breathing new life into the broken. Most of it is wood, which I love, I'm not much into the gleaming plastic and glitter that seems so abundant. However, I cannot seem to escape this twig of a thought in the back of my mind...the shadow that hovers behind the crowd. Do I own, or am I owned?

Fairy Ire

My Dearest Brennan,

I'm on my way to Toledo where there was an unfortunate accident involving a soccer ball and a nine year-old's face leading to his immediate need of payment for not one - but THREE teeth. I must say, I skipped your house last night because just when I was about to open your window, I heard you tell your brother that you no longer believed in the Tooth Fairy! You swore that you saw your mother sneaking out of your room last month with the note in her hand. (*Remember? When you accidentally swallowed your tooth at lunch with your peanut butter sandwich so you had to write me a letter and draw a picture of it? By the way, smashing picture of a tooth!*)

Anyway, I want you to know I skipped you and your tooth last night because you hurt my feelings. *sniff* How on earth could you *possibly* believe that your mother - who usually has a glass of wine or two by 10pm - could actually make it in and out of your booby-trapped room without waking you up? (*yes, I know all about the ropes and nets - do you really think you can catch a fairy?*) However, you most *certainly* would catch your dexterously challenged mother should she venture in to check on you....and then she might have to spend like an hour and a half trying to reset the traps while giggling so hard she brained herself on your dresser, tripped over your skateboard, and landed in your lego box where the space man made a most interesting bruise on her hiney...all *hypothetically*, of course, should she attempt to go in.

Yes, well, you'd better stop all this nonsense about not believing in me - next time I might not be so forgiving. Your mother called me this morning and told me you were sorry, you owe her ***big***. Like I think you should take out the trash for a week...and clean your room. And maybe make her a card.

Much love,
The Tooth Fairy

Amazing....and Elusive Grace

Mercy. Clemency. To pardon the undeserving. The act of forgiveness. How often in our somewhat careless society to we ask for grace? Weekly? Daily? For some, hourly? As we stumble over each other's feelings, drop the proverbial ball, or mishandle our responsibilities - we apologize. We explain. We excuse. But is this the same as grace?

"Giving grace" is forgiving one who has NOT apologized. (*either by choice or opportunity*) There is no groveling, no begging or bootlicking. No atonement...no reparation. It's the driver that cuts you off at the exit. The abhorrently rude woman at the bank who jumped line and then gave you "the look." The market cashier who dropped your carefully chosen, bruiseless golden apples into the bag like pond stones ensuring them to be a brown mottled mess tomorrow.

I do actually forgive easily. I'm the one who always has a "perhaps" waiting to eradicate blame. "Perhaps he's late to the hospital and his wife is having a baby." "Perhaps she has a migraine." "Perhaps they're lost..." From the irresponsible to the downright ill-mannered, I can usually come up with a possible explanation for "why" whatever thoughtless event has occurred.

With. Others. And therein lies the mess. I don't, I cannot, I am seemingly *unable* to give grace to myself. Floating in this vast sea of love and forgiveness - I am choking on self-recrimination, drowning in personal disparagement. The repeating reel playing over and over in my mind, what I *could have said* or *should have done*, becoming a mantra that deafens reason, mutes anything even resembling sweet intangible grace. It matters not the *size* of error...just that it was *mine*.

I am not alone. Within this quagmire of culpability I have much company - mostly female, I admit. Is it in our chromosomes? Our blood? I do know men who feel intense guilt, but usually not for the eons that my fellow women seem to suffer. The masculine ability to wrap the situation up in a neat package, tie it with string, and tuck it away in "storage" stuns me. How do I learn this? Is there a class I can take? Can we start a support group? "Love Thyself..."

I've always known that grace was elemental - irrevocably essential - in every relationship. And yet I am surprised to discover at this point in my life, that this is also true of myself. And so, as this holiday season is approaching simply *loaded* with opportunities for faux pas, disasters & mishaps, I am determined to be gentler to myself. More understanding.

Sometimes I actually do have a screaming headache after an exhausting day and I know there's a stain on my sleeve and I burned the pastry and I've completely forgotten the directions to the party.

A Surprising Sparsity

Crossing off the last item on yet another legal pad list, the black scratch across sunny yellow paper inordinately pleasing, I have shuffled another step closer to Christmas. I am indeed a most advanced addict of lists and all things enumerated. I'm unsure of what birthed this undeniable need for organization within my soul - was it nature or nurture or just a knee-jerk survival mechanism kicking in after enduring traumatizing years with roommates and a first husband that lost their rent, their keys, and their jobs on a disturbingly regular basis. Whatever the case, I do *so* cherish my lists and the peace of mind that comes with them. But once more, there is a yet...

So as is common in our dinnertime routine, I swirled the merlot in my glass, crossed my legs and leaned back in the one of the tall, deeply cushioned chairs that surround the dining room table. Watching the boys finish off piles of roasted green beans with almonds and feta, grilled chicken, and slabs of buttered bread, I asked,

"So Brennan, what was the most fun you had all day?" He took a sip of milk, tilted his head while he thought, and then enthusiastically,

"Oh, when I got to stay in and play on the computer with Kyle for recess!" I laughed, that boy and his computers!

"And you?" I asked his brother. Sawyer finished his bread, considering.

"In gym I caught seven balls during scatterball!" I grinned

right back at him. My oldest redheaded son may not be the biggest of the three, but he's like a monkey when flying through the air and a cat at landing on his feet. The music played on, a piano holiday mix that I love, and Brennan looked at me, a question in his eyes.

"What's the most fun you had today mom?" I chuckled, standing to pick up the empty platter and dishes,

"Well, honey, I got nearly everything done on my list." He wrinkled his nose at me.

"And that's fun?" He was clearly dubious. "Well.....um....." He stood to take his plate to the kitchen, shaking his head. "You should do more fun stuff mom." I gazed after him, unsure how to reply.

The boys had run off, returning to their pre-dinner activities. My husband was working late, so I put a different disc on to play, poured another glass of wine, and finished clearing the table. My kitchen is small - more so than you can imagine, trust me, and there is a lovely porcelain sink but no dishwasher to be seen. I stood, filling the basin with warm soapy water, watching the last of the light flee before the night beyond the skeletal trees. My reflection in the window glass slowly solidified as the sky darkened outside. And then it was just me and myself in the small room, hands submerged, the clink of dishes and the whisper of running water joining my thoughts for company.

Is fun the same thing as satisfaction? A delicious meal, the laundry done, floors vacuumed and pantry full...satisfaction, definitely. Contentment and gratification and peace of mind - absolutely. But fun? I dare say that I consider it part of my "job" as a home-maker to keep the house well-stocked in every way, but I rather dread shopping of any kind. There is no real "fun" to be had playing bumper carts with sale-crazed women and waiting in lines that seem more appropriate at an amusement park; and then there is the hefting it into the car and lugging it all home alone, a million trips back and forth. But I do love that my husband doesn't have to run to the market when he's home, and that there is always another box of tissues and enough bread for a sandwich. I take pride in this, but I don't really consider it 'fun.'

I do delight in cooking, although once again it is perhaps more in the shining eyes and "Mmmm's" around the table that I find enjoyment. I revel in food and am thrilled that this has been contagious within our family - for his twelfth birthday, my youngest has requested my smoked salmon. Not pizza or burgers, but luscious pink flesh brined overnight and then slowly smoked with mesquite chips in a Japanese bamboo steamer - I do absolutely find joy in this. But is it fun?

And then there are the pleasures of the flesh. Warm skin and desire and the flicker of candlelight. The texture of soft hair, the scent of attraction, the taste of passion. While I think I will certainly place this under "fun," should I have "more" of it, I fear I might not accomplish much upon that list...

The dishes dripping quietly, the music faded away. My wine and I curled into the end of the leather couch, marveling at the golden glow of fairy lights and sparkle that is our Christmas tree. The nutcrackers tucked amidst the greenery on the mantle, the candles burning atop the old stereo cabinet that holds the television, its doors now closed. There is such fulfillment here, in the hush and pause after the list is done. But fun?

Do you suppose "fun" is a part of childhood? No, that cannot be true as I have friends that have sporting good fun on a regular basis. In the glimmer of the evening, I am left with just me. I think I will ponder this more. Face the possibility that I have let the responsibility and organization of adulthood consume too much of me...that I have forgotten to include 'fun' on my list.

I believe this Christmas, I shall re-write a list. Or two.

Bread and Friendship

I nearly had a heart attack reading an ice-cream label today...it had 27 ingredients. *Twenty-seven.* I have few addictions. Good martinis, butter...lobster. (*hmmm...some of those certainly go together*) The smell of paint and sunshine...herbs. I subscribe to a single magazine - Saveur. Honestly, I can immerse myself for hours in pages of wild chanterelles, lemongrass, and olives; luscious ideas of tantalizing taste and scrumptious possibility. Last month they had 14 recipes for bloody marys and chocolate gravy! Yet there seems to be a single remarkable theme - real food. Untainted.

We pay a dollar more for the mac and cheese that *doesn't* have "yellow #12" in it; even more for free range chickens fed on grains and worms and grass. We buy jars of peanut butter that only last a month and I am obsessed with my butcher who actually cuts my steaks in front of me - two inches thick and marbled enough to make me bite my lower lip and inhale softly in anticipation of the tender feast that awaits.

The age of MSG. It put american-chinese food on the map – and yet is now the number one anti-advertisement: "delicious with no msg!" Tv dinners, microwave magic, cereal that "has a full day's vitamins in one bowl." (*shudder*) As our technology surged, we reveled in our modern intelligence, our clever short-cuts to facilitate a new world with a new definition of family. No longer was it even *feasible* to awake with the dawn and mix and knead the yeast into loaves that require 6 hours on the back of a warm oven to rise and then bake. Instant was good...filling was better. We applauded, we rationalized. And then. There was this slow...missing.

Like a summer's night without fire flies. Autumn without leaves, Christmas without stockings. Blame it on doubts, on science, disease scares...on texture. We found ourselves with plastic trays and mushy pasta, mediocrity leaving us hungry ten minutes after the meal for lack of flavor alone. The epic death of taste buds.

Why does it seem as we now submerge ourselves in a sea of organic and natural and pure...that we have somehow escalated the fraudulent lives we lead? We rave over unpasteurized goat cheese and fire roasted lamb with figs while we permeate our relationships with additives, enhancements, and garnishes. Our media, our politicians, our families. I have found myself smiling at a party even as I swallowed garish sallow compliments. I've entertained complete frauds. I've been guilty of accepting the synthetic. I've even dished it out...with cilantro.

It seems that the real, the pure relationships are...sparse. Is it just that I'm older? More discriminating? Less patient? As I muddled garam masala and fresh garlic in a mortar and pestle this afternoon, preparing to sear and roast, I found myself contemplating my recent dissatisfaction in my personal relationships. I have rushed. I have microwaved entirely too often. I have settled for instant.

Friendship - real and true and honest friendship...needs yeast, not baking soda.

Mattering

The house was cold this morning when I rose. I'd been awake since three or so - sleep has never been a close companion of mine, especially in these last few years. I spend those dark hours sifting through thoughts and memories. Planning the day ahead and rehashing things I should have said or done differently the day before. Excessive wishing occurs. I suppose these hours spawn much of my writing and should be credited with the seeds of paintings, recipes, and essays alike…but they've also left me with entirely too many hours to flay the flesh from my own bones at times.

The stairs creaked as I made my way down by the light of the small Christmas tree in the entryway. The larger one in the living room, along with the lights on the mantle and across the top of the bar gave most of the first floor a soft warm glow despite the rather arctic hard flooring beneath my bare feet. I nudged the thermostat up, poured a cup of coffee *(thank goodness for pots you can set the night before - almost like having a wife of my own - hot coffee ready at 6am is a marvelous thing)*, and stood looking out the kitchen window, the world icy and frosted white beyond the glass. The boys have reveled in the snow these last few days. I must admit I do not share their delight, winter makes me long for blankets and hot toddies.

I listen to NPR *(national public radio)* as I get ready every morning. I find it much more informative and less irritating than television with its persistent commercialism and tendency to qualify the "latest trend in socks" and "recipes for your holiday brunch" as "news." NPR brings the Middle East into my kitchen, wars and tragedies as well as triumphs and joy - things which help me keep perspective. I fear there is a vast population out there absorbed only in the three square miles that surround them.

Throughout the programming, they often mention famous birthdays. Tidbits of interesting lives. Remarkable moments. Today, it turns out, is Stan Lee's birthday. As the announcer read through several facts about the man, there was near reverence in his voice. It was obvious that Marvel and all of the magic contained therein had touched his own life personally. Spiderman Halloween costumes and Iron Man underroos, a full-color childhood of imaginary champions. As I traced the curve of my lashes with eyeliner, I found myself wondering at a life so...huge. Lee literally altered the world. He poured enchantment into the mundane, created heros with vulnerability as well as strength, made us all believe good would really win in the end and that no matter how desperate the situation, it was still possible to be rescued. *(and this aside from contributing to an industry that encompasses movies and books and careers for thousands)* Stan Lee *matters*. Running my fingers through auburn curls, I clipped the silver hoops into my ears and thought about my day ahead. Would it matter?

Seven hours at the office, home to cook dinner, maybe a stop on the way for some New Year supplies, nothing remarkable. *At all.* Nothing life changing for anyone. Don't get me wrong, I know the boys will appreciate being fed and should I not stop for cheese and peppers, there would be no dip for the mancave sleepover planned for New Year's eve…but do I *matter*? My tiny carved out niche in the world: three boys, an old house; a husband and one neurotic dog. I don't change the world. Far from it. My presence wouldn't register two lines in the local paper, much less a birthday announcement on the radio given with admiration and awe.

It's strange, this world. When I think of the larger pieces of the pie, the names known by all that fabricate and shape the direction of this never ending story we all live within - I cannot help but wonder at the power of the rest of us. Leading quiet lives in quiet homes, giving birth and laughing and weeping and quietly dying. Perhaps it's just the New Year, facing the end of last, resolutions and realizations and such. Perhaps I'm just tired today. Perhaps I need to be more intentional.

Perhaps mattering…doesn't really matter.

Glitter and Ribbons and Wrapping Paper of the Soul

Leaden skies draped my world in dewy garland today. Even now, the rain is still sliding down the windows as the street lights flicker on beyond, their halos misty in the night. Christmas twinkles along the edges of my sight, the fairy lights draped across the bar, the holly piled high atop the china hutch, the buffet littered with half-drunk bottles of wine and a dozen glasses among the poinsettias and candles. Our holiday bash crept up so quickly, my month of novel writing just ended and I had but a week to deck the house and bake the nibbles to delight; a week of ladders and lights and hanging the Moravian star. Ribbons that swirl and stars that spin in the pine-scented drafts...oh, how I love Christmas!

The house is so quiet now. The first day without a scribbled list on legal pad yellow paper, each item crossed off with satisfaction and the last with utter exhaustion. The first day without a deadline except dinner - and bacon wrapped pork chops with lemon and sage make for patient mouths, willing to wait however long it takes. I curled up with a cup of cinnamon tea this afternoon and watched the slate colored sky, recollecting moments of hilarity and joy during the party, as well as several of frustration and fatigue in that week leading up to it. Entertaining is a creature born of effort and organization; it dares you to reach higher, try harder, and do it while ever smiling.

I've been known to joke that I only entertain after dark as candle light is the most flattering, hiding the flaws and imperfections in this ancient house - thus every room is lit with their flickering glow. I passionately adore the character of the old and weathered but as I hung the wreath to cover the crack in the wall, tied the lights to hide the chipped mantle, dangled the ornaments from the dining room chandelier to draw the eye away from the unfinished ceiling, I was reminded of...myself.

The eyeliner to distract from the shadows that hover beneath, lipstick to cover the weariness, a smile to counteract the anger that can be read in the clench of my jaw. Baubles to glitter at my ears, my hair twisted and tucked into shape. Sometimes I feel I wrap and decorate myself much as I do a gift, only I am unsure if it is to prolong the surprise of the wonder inside - or to conceal the defects and disappointments. Each of us fights our own battle to accept ourselves, this I know. Under a barrage of advertising that encourages lifelong dissatisfaction and a hunger for bigger, better, lovelier and sparkly...thinner, smarter, faster. Perpetual reckless improvement.

This holiday, our entertaining now done for the most part, I'm looking forward to quiet nights and peppermint spiked cocoa. Long afternoons in my painted clothing perhaps working on a new canvas, my hair damp from the shower, my cheeks pale in the light. I'm hoping to be more honest with myself, more realistic with my energy and time. More genuine with my emotions. Let us fight the rabid dog of commercialism and comparisons. Let us enjoy each other while resisting the unattainable myth of perfection.

Here's to unwrapping our souls...may we cherish what we discover.

Vulnerable

There is a moment every year when I realize I've lost the sun. As if the frozen air has plucked every ray from my flesh, scraped away summer's glow with icy claws, leeched the color from my skin. Perhaps it's a redhead thing, this day when you notice that you've passed on from ivory and now are somewhere closer to alabaster. Just a notch or so from transparent. Oh, how I do miss the feel of warm rays spilling over my bare shoulders and down my back! *(Spring, please hurry!)*

At any rate, the other night I was sitting next to one of my boys and discovered him staring at my hand.

"Mom," he whispered, "I can see your pulse." I chuckled and told him now he could be sure now I wasn't a vampire - he grinned, but looking at the back of his own hands, he shook his head. "My hands don't have those veins." I ruffled his hair,

"Well love, that's because you're young, perhaps you won't have hands like mine." He seemed slightly disconcerted by this, my youngest and I have much in common, but his brother called and off he ran to play.

Evening was approaching, afternoon's light beginning to fade as the night drew near. I sat in the dusk, swirling the wine in my glass, marveling a bit at the contrast of my pale skin against the crimson liquid. You could plainly see blue lines, veins tracing the length of my fingers, across the back of my hand, disappearing as they swirled around the bones of my wrist. I've always been lucky as far as needles go. A slightly bizarre thing to say, but having such a surface bloodway means that the one in the crook of my elbow is raised up, as thick as a pencil, it cannot be missed. *(it always thrills the nurses - once I had a doc ask if I would come in to let the new aides train on me. Um.....no.)* But such things are not without peril. I have my mother's veins. How strange to stumble across a memory tucked long ago into the eves of my mind...

    I was about seven or so. Mum was drying dishes with me, taking care of the more fragile ones. I remember us just chatting on, and there was a clink. One of the large wine glasses had broken... with her hand inside of it. I remember the scarlet spray that hit the wall in front of us. The pulse of it that was her heartbeat seen, like a mad macabre sprinkler. That split second where my mind added up the volume and the throb of it all and arrived at how serious the injury must be - and for the first time, there in our kitchen with the green ivy towels, my mother became mortal. This superhero who ran our farm with an iron hand, could fly through the door snatching a loaded gun which hung on a rack above each, and cock it with deadly accuracy before even hitting the ground outside - suddenly before my eyes, the bulletproof super woman bled....a lot.

    She wrapped her hand in a kitchen towel, it was soon soaked. As I've mentioned, our land was a long way from any doctor's office. I remember sitting in the passenger seat as she fumbled with the keys...and then stopped. The towel was dripping and there was no way she could drive. Back inside, she called for help and wonderful friends rushed like madmen to our side. They whisked her off and a few stayed with us girls; my father had a moment of sheer panic when he arrived home to a blood drenched kitchen and a house full of people, but all was soon explained. There were stitches and a bandage and that evening, lying in my bed long after dark, I knew my mother was safe upstairs. But invincible no more.

The things that shape us. Ideas and dreams and memories. Do you know, I've never once put my hand inside of a wine glass to dry it? I am stronger than most people I meet. I am six feet tall and have a 36 inch inseam and own my own heavy bag. But the truth remains, every superhero has a kryptonite. A chink in the armor, an Achilles heel. A broken heart, nightmares, shattered hopes, lost causes.

Beautiful humanity, we are so strong. And vulnerable.

Deathswitch.com

It's a lazy Sunday evening. Dusk has settled, turning the bleak white world outside into a sea of diamonds refracting the prism of the streetlights. If I hold my breath I can hear the faint tic-tic of icy crystals on the window glass. I'm waiting for the kettle, listening to the gentle murmur of the radio that eternally plays on in my kitchen. I'm one of those people that rises to coffee and music; take them away and you lose me. I spend hours alone in this room, roasting and basting; with flour on my nose and the scent of fresh basil and lemons lingering on my hands. I absorb the world through the voices that keep me company. As I stand lost in the swirl of my own thoughts, something slices through...a phrase captures me.

Deathswitch.com. Quite a remarkable idea actually. It's a service of sorts. The tag line of the site, "Bridging Mortality." It promises to pass on critical information should you perish unexpectedly. You create an account and begin the process of writing letters and attaching files. To your boss and co-workers: passwords and information. Loved ones, family: they suggest final wishes, bank account information, love notes...and unspeakable secrets.

What would I have to say? If I knew I had only tonight - that dawn would bring my death. What letters would I write? To whom? What have I left unsaid? The crushing weight of conviction then, it dimmed the icy light outside. I looked down, tracing the pattern on the edge of my empty mug. More has remained unspoken than should.

The hours of the night left me time to examine this. Why has this compilation, this pocket of unvoiced thoughts and anger and sadness and love - why have I let it accumulate so? As I sifted through memories, I lingered over ones still tender. Life does indeed persist - despite our deepest wishes in the midst of anger, pain or devastation. Even perfect joy doesn't last no matter how I clutch and cling. The ocean of minutiae surges daily to engulf us in waves of living. We breath, we eat, we lust, we fight, we love...and we leave so much unspoken.

This site, you set your "check-in" times - daily, weekly, once a year. If you miss a check-in they will attempt to contact you. After a period of time, your "death switch" is triggered and the letters sent. Watching the light of the new day creep through the trees, I wonder how people decide to wait, to hold onto these things that are critical enough that they must endure past their final breath. I wish I could read some. What naked honesty must lie in the digital memory of that site. What insight into the soul of regret and repression. What is so vital and yet simultaneously trivial that you can *live* without it being spoken...but you cannot die that way?

The house is chilly. The sounds of early morning surround me - groggy children, the distant thud of a closing drawer. The cat wants out. I brush my teeth. Pushing the sleeves of my robe up, I wash the night from my skin. And I stand there. My reflection with no make-up, no gloss, no pretense. My hair tangled from slipping into bed with it damp, my faded freckles visible. Not as the world sees me...but how I truly am, just me. I'm appalled that I have an unspoken file. I believe so strongly in honesty with love and truth with integrity....and I have been mute.

The gurgle of brewing coffee draws me downstairs, ruffling Noah's hair as I pass. I will tell him...that the point of the lecture - *of every lecture* - is just that I love him. I will write my sister and assure her that the pain of our childhood has passed, and though perhaps not believed, I'm done with it. I will whisper into my husband's ear that petty arguments are never worth missing a single night of the bliss I find in his arms. Cherish my neighbors, appreciate more...confront.

I will de-activate my death switch.

Beyond the Framed

I was browsing through the artwork at a lovely shop recently. There was a couple next to me also clicking through the frames, commenting on such and whatnot. He seemed slightly bored, she alternated looking with picking lint off her black cable sweater. Suddenly she exclaimed,

"Oh, here it is! I've always wanted this for the hallway!" Triumphantly, she placed the coveted prize in her cart with a smile the Cheshire Cat would have admired. There, encased in lacquered dark cherry wood was the familiar scripture, "Love is patient, love is kind. It does not envy...." Nearly everyone could quote this; it's amazing how truth is passed on and repeated and eventually written in lovely calligraphy, framed, and hung upon a wall.

I didn't find anything to captivate me so with my basket on my arm I headed toward the check-out, thoughts of something grilled and cheesy filling my hungry mind. Shifting from foot to foot, we stood. It seemed like there were twelve of us, but I'm sure it was only my imagination. And then I hear a voice - the same voice - demand a spot ahead of me.

"I was here before you!" the lady in black exclaimed, pushing her buggy into another cart, knocking it into the magazine display and causing the "5 Hour Energy" shots to totter dangerously atop it.

"Um, I don't think so." The other cart owner replied, somewhat hesitantly.

"Oh no," Mrs. Black responded, "I'm CERTAIN I was here

first, I was just getting a water over there!" It was late. Everyone in line was hungry, *(the collective sound of stomach growls was beginning to soun*d *like a wolf pack)* and buggy owner #2 just didn't seem up to a brawl with Mrs. Black. *(granted, she did look rather intimidating with her hair sprayed so stiff it resembled a helmet to enter battle with)* And so we stood longer, staring at the back of a black sweater still flecked with lint.

I nestled my bags in the seat next to me, gazing out across the parking lot. The click of the ignition, shift into gear and ease out into the evening traffic. Winter seems murkier this year. Wetter. The holiday lights glittered like stars as I drove home that night. And within me, a fire burned. I'm a redhead. I own a heavy bag. There is a reason.

I spent several years in my twenties down in Guatemala and Mexico. Working with local churches and orphanages, we helped American college kids to come down and work for several months at a time. We built houses, cleared fields, and swabbed scraped elbows and knees in health clinics. We lived in a large cinder block building with a tiled floor. There were no rugs. No television. No hot water. We had a chess board and a radio and a crazy kitten we had rescued named El Tigre, who ate holes in my socks and chased the roaches.

The only "art" in the living room, was on north wall where someone had taken a black marker, and written that scripture. "Love is patient, love is kind..." However, there was another wall. And upon it was written the first three verses of that chapter in the Bible that come directly before the "love is patient" section. The first three seem to be forgotten. Lost. They are not quoted nor have I ever seen them framed.

> *"Though I speak with the tongues of men and of angels, but have not love, I have become sounding brass or a clanging cymbal. And though I have the gift of prophecy, and understand all mysteries and all knowledge, and though I have all faith, so that I could move mountains, but have not love, I am nothing. And though I bestow all my goods to feed the poor, and though I give my body to be burned, and have not love, it profits me nothing."*
>
> 1 Corinthians 13:1-3

Though you have glorious speeches, wisdom and knowledge beyond the ages, invincible faith. Though you give *everything* to the poor and martyr yourself/time/resources...but have not love?

You. Are. Nothing.

I am saddened...I am enraged, by people that know the words. They know the language and they know how to write checks and volunteer at the shelter and adopt a pet. But love? I'm not sure love lives within them.

Love was the only language I could speak in those countries. I remember holding a little girl's hands while they stitched her shoulder back together with minimal anesthetic...and I sang to her. In English. She didn't understand a word that I said, but as tears sluiced down both of our cheeks, she knew love.

This year I am challenging me. I am challenging you. To

analyze your heart. Why do you do what you do? Ian Percy said, "We judge others by their behavior. We judge ourselves by our intentions." He nailed this with caustic accuracy. We constantly evaluate what others are doing, but often excuse ourselves because of our rationalizations, our justifications....our explanations. "I cut that guy off in traffic because I was late." "I snapped at the cashier because I had a bad day." "I had to because my husband was waiting." But even when we do good...do we expect a thank you? Is it for the tax write-off or the applause? Is "love" and *everything that word encompasses*, something you plan and act out? Or does it simply live inside you? In your pores, your breath.

    Love isn't always thanked. It isn't particularly clean. It isn't comfortable and rarely convenient. It's often in the smallest of things. The most overlooked gestures. But when the God of the universe planted the seed within us, the magnificent potential that is the human soul...it was meant to love. Above all, before all, and without filter.

    Without love...we are nothing.

"We aren't the things we collect, acquire, read. We are, for as long as we are here, only love."

A.J. Fikry
A Storied Life of A.J. Fikry

Living in the Two Percent

Because 98% of the time, everything is just fine…

The following are journal entries from this
fragmented, terrifying portion of my life
that changed everything.

4.2.2014

April Fools

It should be unlawful to deliver such news on the first of April. Even as my hands trembled chopping onions, dinner prep my frantic grasping at a straw of normalcy; the sound of my heart thundered in my ears and my mind raced and jerked about seeming to literally crash into the bones of my skull…even then, I still hoped there would be another call. "April fools!" they'd yell and my pulse could slow its mad thrashing within my skin. The earth might find its orbit again.

My husband has a tumor inside his brain. One centimeter by two centimeters seems so small until you are sitting on the edge of a chair staring at the comparative size of his head as he slowly repeats the doctor's words, the black phone gripped in his hand shaking from the earthquake within. It's 'fast growing,' pressing on the part that controls memory, deforming the shape of his brain. This placement can trigger early alzheimer's or ALS.

The world tilted.

Make dinner, listen to the boys chatter, the clang of dishes, dog food in the bowl, laundry up the stairs. I took my shower first, locking the door and turning the taps numbly. The hot water sluiced down my skin, warming flesh so cold. The sobs I had clenched within me for hours began to escape, twisting my spine, wrenching me to my knees in the tub. The plastic liner ripped from the rings and I watched as evening fell and water pooled on the floor.

Was ever a night so long? Crammed with the unknown…my body clutched in his arms, his even breathing in my ear waging war against the chaos of my mind. Dawn came slowly, dragging her damp fingers across the wet sky, the steady patter of the rain finally slowing my heart.

The boys have left for school. Alone, the window beside me frames a world that weeps. Yesterday, while pruning the roses, an inch-long thorn sank deep into the middle knuckle of my left hand. Red and swollen now, it aches; some infection begun beneath the surface perhaps. I flex it over and over as I sip my lukewarm coffee, relishing the corporal pain that holds the agony in my heart at bay. There are days when my dreams seem to follow me into the light, grasping the hem of my nightgown with talons of mist, muddling the line between the real and not as if the night might seep through the membrane of the conscious world and stay for a time. There are things we think and fear that are never said aloud. Unspoken, as if breath would give them life. We cram them into the back of our minds and slam the door, locking those nightmares behind the prison bars of the dark, the unconscious. In this fallen world where evil lives and havoc plays, sometimes there is a prison break. And the nightmare rides into the daylight…the sun on its back, daffodils crushed beneath its hooves. On the first of April.

4.4.2014

Hair

We've known for four days now. Ninety-six hours...well, the doctor called at 4:06 so technically, as I type, ninety-one hours and eleven minutes. It has poured for the last forty-eight or so, spring arriving in a whiplash of wind and rain. My skeleton aches and yet I cannot seem to decide if it's the barometric pressure changes or my fear that is twisting the bones beneath my flesh.

He actually had to go to the hospital where the MRI was taken and retrieve it, deliver it in person to the neurologist's office. I cannot imagine what that was like - passing the shiny disc with images of the monster in his head off to the petite blond woman who now is going to play such a role in our future. We're waiting for her to call...and the waiting is hell.

No one knows except my sister and my parents, and those sentences that tumbled from my lips in shattered panic were followed by, "don't call me." I cannot speak of this aloud. I want no platitudes or reassurances or scriptures. No hugs, no pats on the shoulder, no theories or suggestions. No one knows how this story is going to end. God alone can tell me it will...end, that is. The how is unwritten. I've always believed passionately in the seasons of life. Hard ones, sad ones, empty ones. Some filled with such joy and laughter. Others not. But each comes wrapped in that age old promise: *This too, will pass.* I am utterly terrified of this season. And more so of its end.

We hardly speak of this. He leaves for work and I bundle the boys off to school. They hug me longer, have asked a few times if something was wrong sensing the dread that has come to haunt the shadows of our home. I've lied. I've made bread and cooked meals and done laundry. He comes home exhausted, white faced. We wrap our arms around each other every time we pass in the hall, the kitchen, the stairway; standing for long minutes with his heart beating in my ear, his face buried in my hair. As if we could meld into a pillar that would stave off this disaster.

Last night I was reading while he channel surfed. The kids downstairs, dinner no more than the scent of pulled pork tacos that drifted with the incense through the room.

"They're going to have to shave my head." he said, never turning away from the tv. I looked up, my heart in my throat. I had realized this earlier in the afternoon when researching common treatment options online. He slowly looked at me, his eyes full of the agony we are not speaking.

He's always had long hair since I've known him, one of those things that I love about him. Ex-military, some might think it a rebellion against the shaved skull of boot camp, but I believe it was part of him discovering himself to be something other than a product of a system he had entered at the raw age of eighteen. There was a flag flown in his honor for something he did in those years that he is unable to talk about. I have it upstairs, the thick triangle framed with a letter from John Heinz thanking him. Those years left scars on him; not just the bullet holes that mandated a full body x-ray before the MRI, but jagged wounds torn in his soul. Healing from such trauma takes much longer than most know.

Since leaving his 'corporate job' four months ago for one in the field, he's let the manicured pony tail grow. His hair is now long and wavy, several inches below his shoulders; just looking at him leaves my stomach acrobatic. I have years of memories of that hair...tangled in my fingers as we made love, beneath my cheek as I slept, combed out straight and damp as I trimmed it every few months.

We've wanted some pictures taken of us for a while now. The kind of thing you talk about over pancakes and then forget on the way out the door to take the kids swimming. After I pressed the sobs that had escaped back into the box in my soul earlier that day, I had written to a friend who is an excellent photographer to see if she was free this weekend. She's not. I wrote someone else. I will keep writing. For some things are more than the sum of their parts.

Sometimes hair isn't just hair.

4.8.2014

Threads

The barren branches on the other side of my window sketch black lace against the granite sky. More rain outside. Inside, I am a hurricane. Gale force winds shriek through my mind, whittling away my sense of normal. Erosion. I forget why I've gone upstairs, leave lights on for hours unnecessarily, dial a phone and am surprised at the voice that answers. Last night when Jason asked how I was doing I lied. And he knew. "I need you to be you," he said, "so I can be me." I understand this so deeply that I am trapping the storm within me...within my showers, within my dreams. My me is coming undone.

The doctor's assistant called yesterday, trying to explain why we haven't heard anything. That fateful conversation on the first of April was based on the Neurologist's opinion, the print-out summary sent from the hospital where his MRI was done. Once our own Neuro got her hands on the images themselves, "she doesn't totally agree with his summary." She is trying to get a consultation with him to compare. That's it. "Doesn't totally agree"......?

I've come to believe that the human soul is a tapestry woven with the threads of this life. God, family, friends. Neighbors and warm french bread and summer cricket concerts that echo as the sun sinks below the rim of the world. Threads lovely, threads dark. We wrap ourselves with them, get tangled up in them, trip over them. And in less time than the heart can beat, we can lunge and cling to a single one.

Hope.

The problem with trying to clutch a solitary thread is that it might hold....it might fray....and possibly, like a garrote wire stretched tight in the hands of Fate, it may slice you in two.

The sun has slipped through the clouds and now casts spiderweb shadows across the keys as I type. I picked up a bottle of gardenia perfume from my dresser this morning, its scent a memory-come-to-life as it was something I used to wear in college. I found it in a thrift store a few months ago, half empty. It made me smile, the fragrance of my past. I sprayed my wrists with it today, the essence swirling around me with faces and voices lush, thick with nineteen year-old dreams and Mandy Pansy laughter. It lingers still, flowers in the air...

And hope in my hands.

4.9.2014

A Thread Becomes A Rope

Stunning, how the air can change in a hummingbird's wingbeat. How words, simple strands of letters strung together with stops and stutters, inhale and pause and blink...and I can breathe again. Reviewing the film, consulting the data, neurologists debate and discuss...it isn't *inside* of his brain.

It isn't going to be easy. A mass next to the brain (BUT NOT INSIDE, NOT INSIDE, NOT INSIDE), causing pressure and still needing removed - but no slicing into the marrow that is the man I married, the essence of him. There is so much still before us, but the sense of relief, the tears that tsunamied as the elephantine weight of fear lifted, its claws retracting from their hold on my spinal column...this I will never forget.

Nine days. Two hundred and sixteen hours of anguish. Re-evaluating, re-prioritizing, re-thinking. Remembering. Praying. Screaming.

Still waiting for phone calls to set appointments that will dictate the months ahead. But I can breathe again. The stars have returned to the sky. A rope from a thread....God is amazing.

4.12.2014

Captured

Today I hung the curtains on the porch. The pink sky bleeds into the indigo of night now, the day cooling quickly - this spring eve yet to ingest of inferno of summer so that it lingers into the star flecked dark.

Sky so blue, she clicked frame after frame as we kissed and laughed. Sitting on the steps of our front porch, the boards beneath my palms familiar and covered with my DNA; this home laced with our sweat and labor and love. I held my breath. I smiled.

The afternoon spent re-summering the outside room I nearly live in once the weather breaks; sea shells unpacked, carpets vacuumed, lights lit. I spent hours busy, hands busy, exhaustion cultivated with the desperation only an insomniac knows.

Steaks consumed, the smoke of the grill still caught in my hair like a hazy memory, here I sit. Toes cold, listening to the street hockey game up the block, my rebellious heart refusing to relinquish a perfect day...a normal day. Almost.

Hugs a shade too long, arms wrapped around my waist as I sudsed dinner dishes slower than need be. A throat cleared as the boys perched on the edges of chairs and he explained...sorta. "It's nothing till it's something." Our new house motto.

But they've noticed. They've caught the shadows along the edges, the blur. It seems my world has lost the crispness it once held. I cling to the first appointment made, the date circled in red, it leers from the calendar on the kitchen wall. I glare in return. In purgatory, we wait.

We will make love and make plans and make believe. We will freeze every moment, no matter how trivial...ink prints in our minds, in our hands, our hearts. Like soul photographs, etched in flesh and time.

4.24.2014

The Waiting Room

One hour and fifty-two minutes until the specialist appointment. I've vacuumed the house and done two loads of laundry, ran to the Good Will so I can stop borrowing my son's belt, hit the deli for hot sausage and cheese, and the grocery for miscellaneous odds and bits. I cleaned the kitchen, wiped down the bathrooms...and vacuumed again. Six cups of tea. Every other sentence I type even now I stand up and pace the dining room, shuffling papers from one spot to the next, stack the books, water the plants.

Waiting is exhausting. It has been this way for weeks now, but as the minutes tick off on the corner of this screen, I feel as if the oxygen is being slowly leeched from the room. I keep blinking, things seem out of focus. Hazel has followed me around for days now, sensing my unrest. She lay at my feet last night as I read the same page in a novel eleven times.

I will drive downtown and pick him up, smelling of sunshine and hard work *(which is such an aphrodisiac to me)* he'll smile and climb into the blazer next to me. We'll park in the monolithic garage at the hospital where I perpetually get lost, my sense of direction seems to have evaporated some time ago. He will want to carry the manila envelope that holds the disc of images and correspondence from our neurologist. I know we'll hold hands when we walk inside, we always do. And then we'll see.

4.29.2014

Eggs

Last night, after an exhausting day spent in yard work that needed to be done before a week's worth of rain blew in, I went grocery shopping with Sawyer. I was weary but his company kept me awake and the stories from his recent Marching Band trip made me laugh despite the fatigue. We went to a store that we don't often frequent, mostly as it seems to me that someone took the components of a regular market and jumbled them all up like children's blocks, dumped out mumble tumble. This leads to asking total strangers where they hid the applesauce and making loops back to find black olives and hot sauce.

It was in the dairy department that I paused, tossing cream and cheese in the cart, we came to stop before the eggs. I was lifting lids, setting aside the ones with cracks and a set that sported several icy orbs, when I heard Sawyer's voice, "Wow, there are so many different eggs - I thought an egg was an egg!" I chuckled, his excitement at nearly everything amusing. He went on, "How big is the difference between a small egg and a large one?"

And my heart seized.

Caught totally unaware, I was suddenly back in the bright, antiseptic white office, the doctor's voice echoing in the tense silence. "A mass about the size of a small egg," he said, "very high up in his neck, deep inside, beneath the brain." He paused for a moment and looked down. "It's against his carotid artery." Clearing his throat awkwardly, he picked up his computer tablet and began typing. "I'm ordering another scan, a CT so I can really see what we're dealing with..." And that was the consult.

I didn't realize I had frozen until Sawyer bumped me, holding out a dozen "small" eggs, "Look mom....mom?" I don't really remember checking out. Routine saves us in moments like this; unload, pile on the belt, say hello, wallet - debit card - smile and thank you. And then habit takes us home.

This morning I made hard boiled eggs for breakfast. I stood with my hip against the counter as the water simmered in the dim kitchen, the sun just slipping up over the horizon somewhere behind the curtain of battleship grey clouds. Rain sliding down the world, watering the grass I planted yesterday.

A single egg is suddenly a terribly large thing.

5.12.2014
There's No Bullshitting God

As I write this, I'm thinking of my sister's graduation on Friday, three days from now. She's worked so hard and done so well - I want her to rock that day with no shadows in it from me.

But there's no bullshitting God.

I am so angry. The kind of wrath that wants to throw things and punch walls and scream until there's no air left in the room. Remember the thread of hope? I know, I know - there is "always hope." I know that everything works out in the end, to His glory, to His purpose - I know this in my mind…but not my heart. A good friend wrote to me that she wasn't going to tell me it would all be ok. The only thing she would say, is that I would get through it. Wisdom can, at times, slice through the flesh and tendons…down to the marrow of it all.

It is larger than they thought. It is in an almost "inoperable location." They want a biopsy right away but they're not sure they have the technology to do it as he needs to be inside a scan machine while they are working. I don't even know what that means. I spread the mustard on his sandwich to take for lunch tomorrow and I stare out the window and my mind skips through unfinished thoughts like a record made of sandpaper.

Do you know, I have the hardest time praying right now. As I know the Lord hears my every thought, my every fear, the shattering terror that ricochets through me every time I think about this...I am trusting that He is here. When I kneel on the tub floor and sob and then put ice-packs on my face so I can tuck the boys in, He's here. When I sit on the brown leather chair in the living room as my husband woodenly repeats the latest doctor update and I feel my heartbeat through an endless tunnel, and the room seems to dim and I cannot breathe… As I watch the creep of green swallow up the sky in the back yard, spring growth daily blotting out more of winter's skeletal trees.....He's here. The world turns and the sun rises and I am disintegrating. I find no words for prayer. No ability to ask. There is static and routine and restless unsleep.

I'm making brownies this afternoon, with coconut and white chocolate in them. The sun filters in through the windows making the house glow....it all appears normal.

But there's no bullshitting God.

5.30.14

Decisions and Demons

The last two months have been a battle waged within the walls of myself. Fear and anger have savaged my sense of balance, frustration strangling peace, my ideas of security nothing more than bloody carnage littered across the field of consciousness. I suppose everyone who finds themselves suddenly thrust into 'the story' feels the same. You know, the one you read online or on the last page of a magazine - the tale of tragedy overcome despite *overwhelming* odds. You hold your breath a little reading the middle of it, your heart beats faster, your palms sweat. Then as you read how they triumphed in the end, you let the air out of your lungs and whisper in the back of your mind, *"Dear Lord, I could never handle that!"* And with a slight internal shudder, you close the magazine or turn the page or get up to make dinner and push thoughts of 'that story' far away.

And suddenly I'm the one in the story. It's my family.

Brennan knows. I'm left trying to figure out how to tell the other two. Jason told him last night after two calls from the school, he was suspended for yelling and flipping a desk when a little shit of a kid took his art pencils and began snapping them in two. I've begun to hate the sneaky bullies of this world with a passion that frightens me some. So Jase sat down with him and had the "there's more going on in this family and your mother is on the edge *(I was sitting on the back porch quietly sobbing into my tea)* and you're not holding up your end of things" talk. Brennan cried. I think there are few things more terrifying for a boy of 13 who's seen/read/heard 'the story' a million different times, than hearing that it's your dad that has a brain tumor and is going to have surgery. I didn't know he was going to tell him...

How do I tell the others? Brennan said that I didn't have to, that he would keep it secret. I feel that is an unbearable burden for a child to carry. I'm stumbling now...dropping the ball. I don't know how to do this.

We were turned down by the hospital we've been dealing with. They said that the procedure he needs is too risky for them, they didn't have someone able to do it. So we spent a week and a half waiting to hear back from three other surgeons. The one that finally accepted Jason as a patient, told us yesterday that this requires a "transfacial approach," that they will have to go through the soft tissues of Jason's face down to the base of his skull.....and he will have to be awake for it. How in the hell do we...*how in the name of anything do we prepare for that??*

It's scheduled for next Thursday, June 5th. The last day of school. I will kiss my boys and shoo them out the door for what is supposed to be a glee-filled, exuberant, end-of-year celebration of a day....but they will know that we're going to the hospital as soon as they leave. How cruel that seems. I hate this story.

6.5.2014

And Then, There's God

Thursday morning, 3:07am. Staring at the shadow box that is the bedroom window, silhouette trees in a silent ballad against the iron sky. Fragments of last night's signing of the living will still linger with the flavor of fear. Sleep has fled from dreams too tangible to endure.

5:54am. Bare feet slap softly on the bathroom tile, the sluice of cold water on my face dripping down the silk of my nightgown, eye contact in the mirror with the frightened soul that is quaking within my chest. Deep breath, cold cereal, smiles and hugs and wave the boys out the door for the last day of pencils and books. Hugs that last longer than usual.

8:23am. Clutch my mum come to stay so the boys will have a smile to open the door and see when they return at noon; someone to cut up the apples and chatter about end of year drama...and then I close the car door, my shoulder rigidly inches from his. We pause in the muted vault of steel and wheels, our breathing echoes in the morning air; the unwritten day ahead a book with too many pages.

Garage parking, registration and elevators and overly warm cramped rooms and waiting. The crystalline moment you whisper your love and watch them wheel him away. The hall was acres long.
Hours pass. And then more. His mother by your side, companionship

in the agony of clockwatching. And then the nurse with the kind face touches your shoulder and you look up, nearly leaping to your feet. She walks sedately towards recovery and you almost step on her heels.

Eye contact and the physical lurch of your stomach as you stumble to the chair at the side of the bed. And he says....

"It's gone."

They intended four insertions of the foot long needle through his cheek to the back of his head. They intended to collect four samples of the solid tissue making up the mass of the large oblong shape that was pressing against the artery of his life. They CT scanned over and over, mapping the shape and contours of the monster that lay there, aligning and planning and adjusting. Needle insertion, excruciating necessity. And then, rather than tissue, the syringe was flooded with fluid. Clear, uninfected fluid. And eyes wide with shock, the 4th ranked surgeon in this field watched with wonder as the container filled and the mass collapsed.

It wasn't a tumor. He's never seen anything like it, this doctor, amazed. Has no idea how or why or what - and there are more scans in the weeks ahead and no promises...

But Jason's hearing came back instantaneously. The final scan shows nothing but normal. My fingers keep slipping as I type this, my tears soaking my cheeks, my chest, wiped with trembling hands. I have no words for this....evaporation of weight.

And then, there's God.

Post Script:

The mass grew back, it appears solid now. As of August 2016 we are in a holding pattern - a cycle of fear, waiting, stasis, and faith. Every six months we scan and test; cold linoleum, sweaty palms, racing hearts. And then we are told, again, it's the same size "roughly," and they don't want to touch it until it "causes changes." And we breathe again. I've learned a great deal about living only in today; what tomorrow may or may not hold is utterly beyond my control, but I will not squander my todays.

Mortality has become an unexpectedly close companion. He stops by like clockwork every six months to remind me that pettiness is a waste of breath and anger leads inevitably to exhaustion. Sometimes he's there when I wake in the night, my dreams twisting and dark; sometimes he helps me rewrite my calendar, prioritizing my hours more carefully than I did before. I used to be terrified of him, but truly, we are mortal indeed. Every day is a gift, and we were intended to love.

Unstoppably, without hesitation, and with purpose.

Summer will soon burst into Autumn's flames, the glory of nature on fire before Winter cloaks the world in silver slumber. I am stronger than I believed I could be – but know this only due to the forge we've survived. Today tastes of tenderness and the dreams of my children and tomatoes ripened in the sun.

May your *Season*, whatever it is, be one of wonder. The breadth and width and depth of what it possible in this life is beyond anything we can imagine.

Grow roots. Feast often. Love daily.

Made in the USA
Columbia, SC
08 May 2018